M000011899

A Mighty Fortress

Meditations on the Sufficiency of God

T. M. Moore

Christian Focus

Christian Focus Publications

Our mission statement –

STAYING FAITHFUL

In dependence upon God we seek to help make His infallible word, the Bible, relevant. Our aim is to ensure that the Lord Jesus Christ is presented as the only hope to obtain forgiveness of sin, live a useful life and look forward to heaven with Him.

REACHING OUT

Christ's last command requires us to reach out to our world with His gospel. We seek to help fulfill that by publishing books that point people towards Jesus and help them to develop a Christ-like maturity. We aim to equip all levels of readers for life, work, ministry and mission.

© T M Moore 2003
ISBN 1 85792 868 7

Published in 2003
by
Christian Focus Publications Ltd,
Geanies House, Fearn,
Ross-shire, IV20 ITW,
Great Britain

www.christianfocus.com

Cover design by Alister Macinnes
Printed and bound by MacKay's of Chatham

All rights reserved. No part of this publication may be reproduced, stored in a retrieval system, or transmitted, in any form, by any means, electronic, mechanical, photocopying, recording or otherwise without the prior permission of the publisher or a license permitting restricted copying. In the U.K. such licenses are issued by the Copyright Licensing Agency, 90 Tottenham Court Road, London WIP 9HE

Contents

For Kevin, Kristy, Casey, and Ashley

That our sons may be as plants grown up in their youth; that our daughters may be as corner stones, polished after the similitude of a palace (Ps. 144:12).

Introduction

'With those that despise music, as all fanatics are wont to do, I am not pleased; for music is a gift bestowed by God.... Next to theology, I esteem and honor music.'[1] Thus Martin Luther summarized his view of music, and offered something of an explanation as to why he, a great theologian and Church leader, devoted a portion of his busy ministry to preparing music for the churches of the Reformation to use in the worship of God. Luther believed that music was an effective means of teaching, second only to Scripture; that it could ennoble the soul and build character; and that it was a great and glorious

1. Quoted in F. V. N. Painter, *Luther on Education* (St. Louis: Concordia Publishing House, 1889), pp. 165f.

outlet for expressing our love for God and renewing our commitment to Him.

Among the many hymns that Luther wrote and set to music none is better known or more beloved than 'A Mighty Fortress'. The inspiration for this majestic hymn of faith came to Luther from his meditations on Psalm 46, a psalm of hope in God's strong presence and trust in His wonderful grace. Borrowing a melody from an ancient liturgical chant, Luther wrote words expressive of his own experience of that psalm in the difficult and tumultuous times in which he lived. At particularly trying times in his ministry he would often turn to his closest friend and colleague, Philip Melanchthon, and say, 'Come, Philip, let us sing the 46th.' There is hardly a Christian alive who has not sung some version of this great song of faith at one time or another.

And yet, to observe some Christians singing 'A Mighty Fortress', as I have often done when leading in worship, one could almost conclude that these people do not like this song. They seem distracted, bored. Hardly a trace of emotion or thoughtful engagement with the lyrics ever comes on their faces. They look around, chat with their neighbor, or simply stare ahead without singing. Do they despise music, and are they fanatics against it, as Luther suggested? I don't think so. Probably what I am seeing is nothing more than a version of 'familiarity breeds contempt'. We become so used to something that exercising ourselves over it again becomes a mere routine, something we engage in mindlessly and without much real conviction. Just as we can become bored with our jobs, weary of some avocation, or tired of the same old food, we can grow bored and indifferent to the disciplines of our faith, including the great hymns. The words lose their meaning and significance; the melodies fail to enthrall; the themes become little more than abstract ideas with no reference to our everyday lives. So we go looking for other hymns, new hymns – lively, foot-stomping, hand-clapping, first-person praise and worship songs, with tunes more like what we're used to hearing every day. There we go. That's it. That's much more satisfying, much more to my liking. I could sing this stuff forever, yeah!

Still happily humming away to 'Kum ba ya' are we? The praise and worship songs we take such delight in today will one day become as wearisome to us as the grand hymns of the Christian tradition that we left behind yesterday, and we will go on a quest for something newer and more pleasing once again. The problem is not with the hymns, especially those that have stood the test of centuries. The problem is with the singers – with us. Singing provides a special opportunity of loving God with our minds, as we concentrate on the lyrics of the hymn; with our hearts and souls, as we allow the melody and lyrics to search the depths of our being, challenge our most cherished convictions, and deepen our faith; and with our strength, as we give our voices in earnest, heart-felt expression to the praise of the glory of His grace. That singing the great hymns of the faith is, for many Christians, something less than such an experience is no fault of the hymns. Rather, it is *our* fault, who have allowed the discipline of hymn-singing to become a mere religious routine, and who are merely going through the motions of religious ritual rather than sincerely expressing the depths of our love for God.

The purpose of this book is to explore the theme of the sufficiency of God for all our needs, and to encourage the reader to draw near to Him in more sincere love and devotion through the use of Luther's majestic hymn, 'A Mighty Fortress'. Based on the lyrics of Luther's hymn – a chapter for each half-stanza – the book develops the message behind those lyrics, what Luther had in mind and hoped *we* would have in mind and would experience as we sang his words. Each chapter intends not so much to expound as to illustrate and reaffirm the message of the four stanzas of 'A Mighty Fortress'. By so doing I hope to lead the reader to a deeper understanding of what it means to know, love, serve, and worship the God Who is our Refuge and Strength, a very present Help in times of trouble.

Each of the following chapters will explore the meaning of one-half stanza of 'A Mighty Fortress'. I have taken them in order so that you can better see the thematic development of the lyric. From a bold statement of God's sovereign-might the hymn descends to a renunciation of fleshly dependence in a world filled with demonic adversaries, then rises to a climactic declaration of confidence in Jesus Christ, the Word of God, ending with an emphatic statement of dedication to His Kingdom. As you meditate on the examples of great saints from Church history and Scripture who lived out the teaching of these stanzas, and as you apply the teaching of the hymn in the 'Think About It' section at the end of each chapter, your understanding of the hymn's message and relevance will deepen, and you will be better able to sing 'A Mighty Fortress' as Luther intended – boldly, passionately, and with real conviction. Indeed, I suggest that you take time at the end of each chapter to sing through the lyric provided at the beginning of the chapter in the light of your study. You should find as you do that those words begin to become more real and meaningful to you, that you can sing each stanza with deeper understanding and commitment, and that this hymn can help you to know the sufficiency of God in new and exciting ways. A concluding appendix will lead you to experience even more of the beauty and power of this enduring hymn by introducing you to settings of it by two great Christian composers of the past.

The melody line of 'A Mighty Fortress' consists of three themes or ideas. The first theme, which carries the first half of each stanza (explored in chs. 1, 3, 5, and 7) is like a trumpet blast, a mighty proclamation of Scriptural truth. Radically disjoined, the first theme covers the whole lyrical range of the hymn, like the declaration of an all-embracing world view. Noted initially at the top of the hymn's tonal register, these lines are intended for bold, emphatic, deeply convicted singing. They verily beg to be shouted. Just consider the message they carry: God is our Mighty Fortress, our Helper! We will not trust in worldly ways or inclinations, for we would surely fall if we did. Christ stands beside us, and we will trust in Him. We expect to be assaulted and assailed in this world, but we will neither tremble nor fall. God's Word can and will sustain us against the attacks of our foes; in Him we will surely have the victory!

These are not lyrics to yawn through, and this is not music to mutter. These lines are a gauntlet thrown down at the feet of the world, the flesh, and the devil, defying their seductive schemes and destructive devices, and proclaiming our full intention of standing firm on the Rock of our salvation, come what may. Here is an opportunity to declare our deepest convictions, the life-and-death beliefs that make us the people of God and set us apart from a desperate and dying generation.

The second theme takes up the middle of each stanza (chs. 2, 4, 6, and 8), is in the middle of the tonal register, and is more reflective, more observant of the realities of life in this world. The melody is more conjunct, inverting in the second half of the theme, almost like someone whose thoughts have gone out in a question and come back with some preliminary resolution: our ancient foe, the devil, still seeks to destroy us, and he's a crafty fellow. Do you ask who can help us against him? Jesus Christ, the Lord of Hosts, that's Who! We're not afraid of the prince of darkness! We can stand up against whatever he might throw at us. Sure, he may take away our wealth, our friends, even our own lives. But God's truth, opened to us and expressed through us by His Spirit, will never fail!

The final theme is the recapitulation or restatement of the initial theme (chs. 2, 4, 6, and 8). Each stanza of 'A Mighty Fortress' ends with a confident re-assertion of great Biblical truth, using the melody line of the ending of the first theme. We begin with proclamation, and each stanza ends with it as well: make no mistake about it, the enemy of our soul is strong. But Christ can beat Him in battle; one little Word from Him and the devil is history! God's Kingdom is forever!

The combination of words and melody in 'A Mighty Fortress' makes this a hymn of great strength, a powerful meditation on the sufficiency of God to rescue, sustain, guide, empower, and deliver us from evil in a world filled with temptations and trials. It is a mighty statement of trust in God and commitment to the cause of His Kingdom. As we sing this hymn we need to let the full significance of its message capture our imagination; the full power of its melody fill the chambers of our heart and soul; and the full strength of its confession become our confession as well. As we do, our sense of the sufficiency of God for all our needs will grow stronger and become more real for us, and we will grow in faith and the joy of our salvation.

I want to thank my wife, Susie, for her constant encouragement as I have worked on this book. In many ways her bold, uncompromising faith represents the very embodiment of all that Luther expressed in this hymn, and of what I strive more and more to know in my own walk with the Lord. May God be pleased to use this book to help us recover something of what has been lost in our worship of God, and to enable us to depend more confidently and consistently on our Mighty Fortress amid the trials and challenges of Kingdom living in the world.

1.

A Mighty Fortress

A mighty fortress is our God,
a bulwark never failing!
Our helper, he, amid the flood
Of mortal ills prevailing.

I have heard of thee by the hearing of the ear: but now
mine eye seeth thee. Wherefore I abhor myself, and
repent in dust and ashes (Job 42:5, 6).

As he sat in chains in the cold, wet bowels of a French
prison ship, John Knox reflected on the events that had
led to his captivity: the eruption of Protestant sentiments
in his native Scotland, the murder of Cardinal Beaton,
his own rise to prominence as a premier spokesman for

the reform movement, and the combined Scottish and French effort to crush the rebellion, culminating in the surrender of St. Andrews Castle.[1]

He had fled to St. Andrews Castle with pupils in tow seeking refuge from those who were determined to revenge the Cardinal's death and return Scotland fully to the Catholic fold. By the time he arrived, Easter, 1547, Knox had already acquired a reputation as a controversialist and outspoken opponent of anything that did not conform to the straightforward teaching of the Word of God. St. Andrews Castle was soon to come under siege, and the leaders of the resistance, believing the people needed an inspiring preacher to bolster their courage for the difficult days ahead, looked to John Knox, calling upon him to assume the role of preacher within the Castle Church. At first he declined, but after reflection took up the charge.

He would become a thorn in the flesh for those who called him to the work. His first sermon, from the prophet Daniel, was appropriate enough, as he railed against the well-known corruption of religion in his day and called on the people to stand firm for the cause of Christ. The leaders of the resistance congratulated themselves that they had found in Knox a powerful popular spokesman

---

1. For a complete account of Knox's captivity, and of his ministry as a whole, see John Knox, *The Reformation in Scotland* (Edinburgh: The Banner of Truth Trust, 1898, 1982), pp. 52ff. See also Lord Eustace Percy, *John Knox* (Richmond: John Knox Press, 1966), pp. 47-59 and Elizabeth Whitely *The Plain Mr Knox* (Fearn, Ross-shire: Christian Focus Publications, 2001)

for the rebellion. But he would prove a disappointment to them. Immediately Knox began to speak out, condemning the moral and spiritual corruption of the 'Castilians', as the defenders of St. Andrews were called, and especially of their reliance on stone walls, military armaments, and friendly governments for their defense. St. Andrews Castle was an ancient and formidable structure, and the leaders of the rebellion were sure it could protect them against their adversaries until the help of the English could be secured. Thus, as a fleet of French warships and galleys entered the harbor of St. Andrews, the rebel leaders urged their followers to the defense of their fortress, calling on them to trust in human fortifications and weaponry to prevail against their foes.

Knox was of another mind. Like Jeremiah in a besieged Jerusalem, he told the people and their leaders that their trust in the instruments of the flesh was futile against God, Who had come to chastise them for their sins. He warned them that 'their corrupt life could not escape the punishment of God'; that was his continual advertisement, from the time that he was called to preach. When they triumphed – the first twenty days [of the siege] they had many prosperous chances – he lamented, and ever said, 'They saw not what he saw.' When they bragged of the force and thickness of their walls, he said, 'They shall be but egg-shells.'[2]

He was, of course, correct. On July 31, 1547, the thick walls of St. Andrews Castle were breached, at the cost of

---

2. Knox, *ibid.*, p. 80.

many lives. What horror and dread must have filled those who had trusted those ancient stones to defend them! The survivors were taken aboard French prison ships where they languished at sea, miserably treated, and with an uncertain future. For many weeks they drifted from port to port, with little to eat and almost no opportunity to see the light of day. Some died in a fire that burned one of the prison vessels – ironically named, The Cardinal. Many fell to unknown fates. Only a few – among them, John Knox – lived to return to their native land and continue the work of reformation they had begun.

Beside Knox in the prison ship sat two of the rebel leaders who had boasted of the strength of St. Andrews' walls. He did not need to speak to them about the foolhardiness of their actions. His very presence was rebuke enough. Where now was the protection of their castle fortress? As the sea buffeted the wooden vessels, and sea water

A mighty fortress is our God,
a bulwark never failing!
Our helper, he, amid the flood
Of mortal ills prevailing.

seeped through the seams into the belly of the ship and around the prisoners' feet, a tide of hopelessness, defeat, and doom rose like a flood in the hearts of many. On what supposedly infallible bulwark would they rely now? What help would these leaders offer their trusting followers, as they languished together in the darkness of their common prison? Had they listened to Knox, repented of their sins, and sought the Lord's will for their defense, who knows what God might have been pleased to do? As it turned out, however, their dependence upon their own wiles and resources, and the stone walls of an ancient man-made fortress – all of which were but symptoms of their cavalier approach to the life of faith – had brought them to this frightful and humbling fate. They had put their trust in the wrong fortress. Now their misplaced faith had turned to defeat, humiliation, and ruin.

If ever a man had reason to find comfort in a fortress consisting of the things of this life, surely it was Job, 'the greatest of all the men of the east'.[3] He was the head of a large and beautiful family, graced with seven handsome sons and three beautiful daughters. Job had known unparalleled success in business: 'His substance was seven thousand sheep, and three thousand camels, and five hundred yoke of oxen, and five hundred she asses,' together with servants and employees to care for all his possessions and to manage his affairs.[4] He was renowned for his moral uprightness, generosity, and wisdom. The sins and shortcomings of ordinary men could not be laid against his charge.[5] On top of all this he was a man of deep and sincere faith, seeking the goodness of the Lord for himself, his family, and all with whom he had to do. Job was as spiritually, materially, and financially secure as one could possibly be; everything was going just right for this greatest of ancient saints.

---

3. Job 1:3
4. Job 1:2, 3.
5. Cf. Job 4:3, 4; 10:7; 23:10-12; 30:25; 31:1.

But there was a weak spot in the walls of Job's fortress, which would only come to light in the midst of a demonic siege of trial and tragedy.

When events in Job's life began to sour, they came not by degrees, but all at once. A terrible storm brought down the house of one of his sons around his children, taking all of them from Job in one devastating blow. Raiders and bandits from nearby kingdoms made off with his property and murdered his servants, bringing his business to ruin and his fortune to naught. In the midst of all this, Job himself was stricken. Horrible boils broke out on his body, leaving him to suffer pitiably. He became a byword to all his neighbors, who wondered aloud about whatever might be the hidden sin that had occasioned all this tragedy. His embittered wife abandoned him. His trusted friends turned against him. None could be found to succor and console him in the midst of his deep and devastating crisis.

The walls of his fortress of success and security had come under demonic attack. Early into his tragedy Job continued to trust in the Lord, confident that God would help him to understand the meaning of these terrible events. In the face of his wife's despairing rejection he asserted, 'What? shall we receive good at the hand of God, and shall we not receive evil?'[6] As his friends counseled him to confess whatever hidden sin had caused these disasters, he continued to maintain his innocence and declared his belief that God would give him the

---

6. Job 2:10.

wisdom to understand the reason behind his undoing: 'Though he slay me, yet will I trust him.'[7] The bulwark of Job's faith seemed unassailable. But events would prove otherwise.

As his self-confident, judgmental friends continued to regale him with charges of hypocrisy and sin, Job answered their accusations with example after example of his righteousness in an effort to deflect their charges and re-assert his innocence. But the more he refuted their explanations of his sore distress, the more he was left without a way of accounting for the terrible events that had befallen him. If he didn't accept their interpretation of things, how would he explain these terrible events? Surely he should be able to make sense of all this? It began to seem to Job that God owed him some explanation. If he himself was without blame, what then? Why had God in His infinite wisdom and power allowed these circumstances to come to pass? Certainly God was sovereign in all the affairs of men, and certainly He had the well being of His faithful people in mind in all He did. Why, then, could Job not figure out what was wrong? Why was this understanding kept from him? And was this right? Was it fair of God to deny so faithful a servant insight into the meaning of all that had befallen him?

The relentless bombarding of the fortress of Job's faith by Satan and Job's own friends had begun to expose a weak spot in the walls. All was well, and Job could

7. Job 13:15.

trust in the Lord as long as he had some hope of being able to make sense of his situation. But that self-assurance, and with it, Job's peace and hope, would ultimately come under attack as well – but from a most unlikely source.

By the time his 'friends' had worn out their welcome, Job had become angry at God for leaving him in the dark. His impatience and sense of outrage got the best of him, and in Job 31 it all erupted in an ugly outburst of indignation against the sovereign God of heaven. Job protested his innocence in all matters (vv. 1-32). He declared the consistency of his confessions and repentance from all known sin (v. 33). He boasted that he was free of the fear of men for the sake of his faith in God (v. 34). Then, rising up from his desperation and despair, Job shook his fist at the heavens and demanded that God come down and give him an explanation for the events that had befallen him:

> Oh that one would hear me! behold, my desire *is, that* the Almighty would answer me, and *that* mine adversary had written a book. Surely I would take it upon my shoulder, *and* bind it *as* a crown to me. I would declare unto him the number of my steps; as a prince I would go near to him.[8]

This challenge was met by one more round of rebukes from a young man who had been standing by, waiting for

8. Job 31:35-37.

the others to exhaust their case against Job. Only after Elihu had finished reporting his own conclusions did God finally appear (chs. 38–41). When He did, He made no attempt to comfort Job or to relieve his intellectual and spiritual distress. Instead, God took aim at the intellectual inner walls of Job's fortress, denouncing his insistence that he should be privy to the counsels of divine wisdom rather than have to trust in God Who alone is infinitely wise: 'Who *is* this that darkeneth counsel by words without knowledge? Gird up now thy loins like a man; for I will demand of thee, and answer thou me.'[9]

The weak point of Job's faith had been exposed. His confidence and assurance were ultimately resting on his own ability to make intellectual and theological sense out of his sufferings. He was trusting in the fortress of his mind, rather than in the sovereign God of heaven and earth. Now the walls of his fortress would be breached by the unremitting bombardments of divine prerogative and prosecution. Job had made the mistake of trusting in his *faith* in

A mighty fortress is our God,
a bulwark never failing!
Our helper, he, amid the flood
Of mortal ills prevailing.

God more than in God Himself! He believed that he was such a man as could understand all matters, a man from whom the Deity would not withhold any information or insight that he needed in order to be at peace. He had believed God all his life, and had prosecuted all his af-

9. Job 38:2, 3.

fairs in a way that was pleasing to Him. Surely God would not abandon him in the hour of his distress. Surely God would show him the reason for his sufferings, so that he might be at peace in his mind, knowing the divine rationale behind his distress. Surely his faith was strong enough to be able to see into divine mysteries and find, through understanding rather than trust, the peace of God that passes understanding. God, Job believed, *owed* it to him to explain the reason for all these mortal ills, so that his mind might be at ease.

Through the breach of Job's presumptuousness the chastening of God poured like a flood. Not even Job's feeble attempt at pre-emptive surrender could forestall the overwhelming of his fortress by the displeasure of God.[10] Only when God had reduced his boastful bulwark to rubble would Job be able to see the full extent of his sin and show the repentance God was looking for.[11] Job had known God at one level – the 'hearing of the ear'. But now he saw more clearly – with 'the eye' – and realized that he had not fully trusted in the sovereign power and goodness of God, come what may. He had made an idol out of his own faith, trusting in his trust in the Lord, and his life of obedience, rather than in God Himself. In repenting 'in dust and ashes', Job expressed his shame at having trusted in his own faith, and submitted in humble obedience and peace to the wisdom and greatness of God, precisely the response that John

---

10. Job 40:3-6.
11. Job 42:1-6.

Knox had hoped for from the Castilians. And with that repentance came the reassuring grace of God to renew, revive, and restore Job, and to put his detractors in their place.

How easy it is for us to depend on things other than God Himself to protect us amid the flood of mortal ills that daily seeks to prevail against us. Loving families, well-paying jobs, secure nest eggs, warm homes, happy churches, even our own intelligence, charm or spirituality – all of these can become redoubts behind which we take shelter when trials or difficulties lay siege to our well being. Yet none of these is a bulwark strong enough to preserve our peace. Only God Himself will do. Only knowing Him, resting in and resorting to Him, and leaving the hard issues, difficult decisions, and mind-boggling uncertainties to His sovereign, loving care will allow us to be completely at peace in the midst of every circumstance, and to know the victorious power of God's presence in our midst and on our side. God alone is our Mighty Fortress, the only Helper Who can keep us from being overwhelmed by the flood or mortal ills that rises against us continually. The challenge to us is to learn how to take refuge in Him, and not in any flimsy redoubts of our own devising.

Luther's majestic hymn, 'A Mighty Fortress is Our God,' declares this confidence in God, encouraging us to cling to nothing in this life, but only to Him. As we saw in the Introduction, Luther was inspired in writing this hymn by his meditations on Psalm 46:

God *is* our refuge and strength, a very present help in trouble. Therefore we will not fear, though the earth be removed, and though the mountains be carried into the midst of the sea; *Though* the waters thereof roar *and* be troubled, *though* the mountains shake with the swelling thereof.

Like John Knox and the other reformers of the sixteenth century, Luther knew fear, frustration, and uncertainty.[12] But he also knew the Lord. More than this, he knew that *knowing* the Lord – loving Him, delighting in Him, seeking Him, worshipping and serving Him – was the only stable ground on which to stand at all times. He wrote 'A Mighty Fortress' to remind himself and those he served that God and God alone is the only unfailing bulwark against the uncertainties of changing times. Goods and kindred would fail them; devils and demons would assail; their own faith would be assaulted and shaken at times. But God is an unchanging, irreducible Fortress. If we take refuge in Him, and rest by faith in Him at all times, we will know the peace that passes understanding and the joy of our salvation.

God is our refuge and strength, our 'Mighty Fortress'. The weapons of our warfare against the forces that would bring us down are not those of the flesh – things, relationships, positions of power and prestige, or even our own moral, mental, or spiritual attainments. They must be the weapons of faith – prayer, fasting, waiting

---

12. See on, chapter 6.

on the Lord, trusting in His Word, obeying His every command, giving thanks and rejoicing in all things. Only those who, laying aside confidence in everything else and exercising unwavering trust in Him, will know lasting, unshakable peace in the face of every challenge and trial in life.

Think About It

1. In prosperous times it can be very easy for us to trust in the many things God has provided us for our sense of happiness and well being. How were the Castilians guilty of doing so? How does the example of Job warn us against this?

2. Trusting in God begins with knowing Him. But we cannot know God apart from knowing and trusting in Jesus Christ, His Son. How do the following passages help us to understand the importance of knowing Christ in order to know God? What does each teach us concerning Him, and what He requires of us?

John 14:6; John 17:3; Acts 16:30, 31.

3. But what does it mean to *know* Jesus Christ? First, it means to understand Who He is and what He has done for us. Look at the following passages. What do they tell us about Who Jesus is and what He has done for us?

Hebrews 1:1-3; John 1:1-12; John 3:16, 17; 2 Corinthians 5:17-21.

4. Do you know Jesus Christ in this way? Those who know Him will *delight* in Him. They will *seek* Him, and want to spend time getting to know Him better. And they will *worship* and *serve* Him throughout the course of their lives. Think about this: What would someone 'look like' who delighted in the Lord Jesus, sought to spend time with Him, and worshipped and served Him faithfully? How would his or her day begin and end? How would he or she conduct their relationships or approach their work?

5. Jesus shows us what it means to flee to the Mighty Fortress of God at the really trying times of life. No matter how terrible or confusing our circumstances, we can show the Lord that we trust in Him and rely on His grace to sustain and provide for us. Psalm 22 gives a striking prophetic portrayal of the suffering of Christ on the cross. Written 800 years before the event, Jesus cited this psalm to stimulate the minds of those observing His death concerning the meaning of that tragedy (Matt. 27:46). In each of the following verses of that psalm, what can we learn from our suffering Savior about how to take refuge in our Mighty Fortress in difficult and trying times? What is the focus of Jesus' prayer in each of the following?

Psalm 22 vv. 3-5; vv. 9-11; vv. 19-22.

2.

Our Ancient Foe

For still our ancient foe
doth seek to work us woe;
his craft and pow'r are great;
and armed with cruel hate,
on earth is not his equal.

Be sober, be vigilant; because your adversary the devil,
as a roaring lion, walketh about, seeking whom he
may devour (I Pet. 5:8).

The journey from Northampton to Stockbridge,
Massachusetts, is only about sixty miles, a few short
days on horseback. But, in the lonely, dark, and unsettled
woods of March, 1751, it must have seemed an eternity to
Jonathan Edwards. He had been asked to consider a call

to the small congregation in that outpost village, and to take up the mission work of reaching the native American population who had shown some interest in the things of Christ. What thoughts must have run through his mind as he made this exploratory visit. Would the people in that frontier setting take to his formal and highly theological preaching and ministry style? Would he be able to learn the native tongues of the Indians to whom he must minister? Would his family be able to adjust, especially since the church in Stockbridge had no parsonage at this time? Would he ever have a ministry blessed of God again?

The circumstances of his separation from the church in Northampton haunted him. Edwards ministered in that town for twenty-three years, during which he led the people to experience two significant seasons of revival, and saw the church grow to over 700 members. Some of his greatest pastoral and theological works date from this period. He had been the beloved counselor, spiritual guide, and moral guardian for the members of the community since succeeding his grandfather, Solomon Stoddard, to the pulpit in 1729. Northampton was the only home that he, Sarah, and their children had ever known.

But in 1750 all that changed, abruptly and cruelly, leaving Edwards without a call, without support, and with an uncertain future. Edwards' view of the Lord's Supper had undergone a change in the years before 1750. Prior to the late 1740's he had followed Stoddard's view, and that of most New England ministers, that the Lord's Supper was a 'converting ordinance'. That is, the practice of New England churches was to leave the communion table open and accessible to all, professing Christians and non-Christians alike, in the hopes that the former would be strengthened in their faith and the latter led to put their trust in Christ through participating in the dramatic re-enactment of His suffering on their behalf.

As he studied the Scriptures on the matter, however, Edwards' view of the Supper gradually changed, until he finally came to see the ordinance as reserved for those alone who could offer a credible confession of faith. His attempt to adopt this practice in the congregation at Northampton led to objection, opposition, turmoil, and, ultimately, his dismissal from the church.

The fight to remove Edwards from the pulpit in Northampton was bitter and much involved, and drew in not only the members and leaders of the Northampton church but pastors and delegates from surrounding congregations as well. The situation afforded an opportunity for wide publication and careful consideration of this theological issue. But it also made a way for jealousy, opportunism, and spiritual pride to infect the congregations of the region.

Edwards argued in preaching and print for his view, basing it squarely on his new understanding of the teaching of Scripture. Long-time members of the Northampton church resented his effort to break with the tradition observed by their beloved former pastor,

Solomon Stoddard. Rival theologians exaggerated Edwards' claims and misrepresented his teaching, so that he came to be charged with perfectionism, and with wanting to establish a pure church; he consistently denied these charges. The debate culminated in Edwards being dismissed from his pulpit and left to fend for himself for the future. Thus the people of Northampton cashiered the shepherd who had given himself to their spiritual welfare so faithfully and sacrificially all those years. While he acknowledged his shortcomings as a minister, and accepted some blame for this debacle, Edwards came to see that all this trouble had come as a result of spiritual pride. He wrote concerning the congregation at Northampton:

> In latter times, the people have had more to feed their pride. They have grown a much greater and more wealthy people than formerly, and are become more extensively famous in the world, as a people that have excelled in gifts and grace, and had God extraordinarily among them; which has insensibly engendered and nourished spiritual pride, that grand inlet of the devil in the hearts of men, and avenue of all manner of mischief among a professing people. Spiritual pride is a most monstrous thing.[1]

---

1. Quoted in Iain Murray, *Jonathan Edwards: A New Biography* (Edinburgh: Banner of Truth Trust, 1988), p. 341. See Murray for a full presentation of the details of this situation.

The devil, Edwards saw, had brought about this unhappy situation by inciting spiritual pride in the hearts of many.[2] In 1760, ten years after the controversy, one of those most outspoken against Edwards, his cousin Joseph Hawley, reached a similar conclusion, and printed a letter in a Boston newspaper admitting his guilt and accepting responsibility

*For still our ancient foe
doth seek to work us woe;
his craft and pow'r are great;
and armed with cruel hate,
on earth is not his equal.*

for his role in Edwards' dismissal. He confessed that he 'was very much influenced by vast pride, self-sufficiency, ambition, and vanity'.[3] The devil, the Church's ancient foe, had made hay in Northampton at the expense of Jonathan Edwards and his family. Apparently he had managed to blind the eyes of Edwards' opponents to the fact that he is ever stalking about, seeking to work woe against the saints of God and to devour whomsoever he may. A fact which the Apostle Peter knew all too well.

Those must have been heady days, those weeks just prior to the Lord's triumphant entry into Jerusalem. His fame and recognition were growing, as He cast out demons, healed the sick, fed and taught the multitudes, calmed the seas, humbled the proud religious leaders, and endeared Himself to the masses. And with the rising tide of His popularity, the visibility of His apostles – and their own spiritual self-images – was being lifted as well.

---

2. *Ibid.*, p. 347.
3. *Ibid.*, p. 348.

Jesus may have sensed as much. At Caesarea-Philippi He examined His apostles in order to make certain that they understood both Who He was and what their callings must entail. 'Who do men say that I, the Son of Man, am?' He asked them.[4] They answered by offering a catalog of the responses they were hearing: John the Baptist come back from the dead, either the prophet Isaiah or Jeremiah similarly revived, or one of the prophets of old. 'Who do you say that I am?' To which Peter responded, no doubt with a confidence that was intellectually far ahead of where his heart and life had yet arrived, 'You are the Christ, the Son of the living God!' Jesus responded with an affirmation asserting such knowledge to have come from God only, and declaring that Peter would play a significant role in building the Church of the Lord.

Peter must have beamed! The Rock! Jesus had called him The Rock, saying that upon such as He would build His Church. How this must have elevated Peter in the minds of his colleagues. Peter, always so impetuous, so ready to leap into the fray on behalf of the Lord. Did the other disciples resent his bluster and bravado? If so, all that would surely be forgotten now, now that the Lord had spoken such words to him.

But in Peter's rising sense of spiritual elevation were the seeds of his humiliation. Shortly after the examination at Caesarea-Philippi Jesus began to explain to His disciples that 'he must go unto Jerusalem, and suffer many things of the elders and chief priests and scribes,

---

4. Matthew 16:13ff.

and be killed and be raised again the third day'. What's this? Suffer? Be killed by the religious leaders of the day? Not, Peter must have reckoned, if I have anything to say about it: 'Then Peter took him, and began to rebuke him, saying, Be it far from thee, Lord: this shall not be unto thee.'

To rebuke Him? To contradict and correct the Son of God, the Christ? Did Peter consider that he knew better than the Lord, and that, if necessary, he himself would stand against any foes or assailants and secure the Lord of glory from any treachery by their hands? Was Peter's insight into the divine plan for the redemption of God's people superior to that of the very Son of God? Did he know better how God's will should proceed than the Word of God incarnate? Where had such brazenness come from?

Jesus left no doubt: 'Get thee behind me Satan: thou art an offence unto me: for thou savorest not the things that be of God, but those that be of men.'

From insight into the nature of Christ to an enemy of the will of God; blessed and elevated to an offense; confessor of the Son of God to henchman of the devil; rock to rubble! Peter had fallen into spiritual pride, considering that he knew better than the Word of God what the will of God must be, and resolving to take the eternal plan of redemption into his own hands if need be in order to ensure the honor of God and the safety of His Son. Peter's adversary the devil had laid a subtle trap, and the well-meaning apostle had fallen headlong into it.

Popular Christian and contemporary culture likes to portray the devil in fiendish terms – rampaging demonic spirits, ghoulish possessors of the unwitting, or slick and subtle world leaders. Be on the lookout for such as these, we are advised.

Peter also warns us to be alert to the wiles of the devil. But the Rock of the Church knew the adversary of our souls to be much more subtle and powerful than the titillating images of pop culture make him out to be. His attacks can be difficult to detect as he comes stealthily under the radar of our fiend-fixations. Satan does indeed stalk about, like a roaring lion, seeking to work us woe.

For still our ancient foe
doth seek to work us woe;
his craft and pow'r are great,
and armed with cruel hate,
on earth is not his equal.

His craft and power are great, and he is motivated by nothing but hatred for God and for the people who call upon Him in faith. And He finds a weak place in the fortress of our faith and a ready fifth-column for his destructive purposes in the spiritual self-esteem of the followers of Christ, who have come to think more highly of themselves than they ought, and who trust in the strength and schemes of men rather than in the Word of God.

The husband who considers that, as the head of his house, he has little to learn about the walk of faith from his wife or children. The pastor, schooled in the latest techniques and sure of his own spiritual reserves, who believes himself impervious to lust and licentiousness in a counseling situation. The church court which bypasses the requirements of love and pastoral care in order to please men or to fulfill the outward requirements of some ecclesiastical protocol. Pastors and theologians who denounce other Christian teachers for some perceived shortcoming in their exposition or confession. These all are prime targets for Satanic subversion.

The Christian witness who smugly destroys his opponent with tightly-reasoned arguments. The church member who ignores the spiritual needs of her neighbor as she flaunts her knowledge of Scripture before the members of her Bible study group. The young person who believes his faith is strong enough to keep him from falling into sin as he dabbles with pornography or sex. The church member who makes a career of correcting the pastor or Sunday school teacher at every opportunity. The council of church leaders that considers the techniques of business management to be preferable to the shepherding ways of Christ in growing the Church of God. The congregation that sets aside Biblical elements of worship for what pleases the dead palates of worldly men and women. All these have come into the cross hairs of the enemy of our souls.

The psalmists speak often of their concern that their enemies should not have occasion to exult over them.[5] How the devil and his spiritual henchmen must howl and dance at every moral lapse of some Christian leader; every unkind word spoken and justified in the

---

5. Cf. Ps. 3:1f.; 13:3f.; etc.

name of the Lord; every bypassing of the clearly revealed will of God for sake of convenience, expediency, 'relevance', or pleasing men rather than God. In many ways the Church of Jesus Christ today is throwing a perpetual party for the spiritual forces of wickedness in high places, as, resting in our spiritual smugness and self-assurance, we countermand, neglect, ignore, rationalize away, or simply deny the straightforward teaching of God's Word, preferring our own plans, schemes, and ideas instead.

Certainly the devil has many, many ways of troubling the saints of God, as we saw in the case of Job. But undoubtedly one of his most potent tactics is that of laying hold on spiritual pride and turning it to his own purposes, allowing us the appearance of spirituality as, in reality, we undermine the cause of Christ. How many of us who have taken the name of Jesus upon us are involved in activities today that will lead us at some point, like Joseph Hawley, to acknowledge that we have been little more than pawns in the hand of our ancient foe? Better to hear the rebuke of the Lord now than to continue warming our hands in the enemy's camp, denying the Lord by our words and deeds – or lack thereof – while we congratulate ourselves on how spiritual we are. Satan's craft and power are great. But the Word of God, our Mighty Fortress, is greater by far. The sooner we learn not to confide in our own strength in all our strivings, but to rest in the clear teaching of God's holy Word, the sooner we will turn the tide of battle against the enemy of our souls and reclaim the high ground in our lives for Christ.

Think About It

1. In the case of Edwards his opponents appealed to tradition and familiar practice, while Edwards argued his case from the teaching of God's Word. Edwards lost. Why do such things as tradition ('what we've always done'), familiarity, what our friends might say, and so forth exercise such a strong hold on what we believe and how we behave?

2. Do you believe that Peter's 'rebuke' of Jesus was well-intended? What must have been going on in Peter's mind? What was he thinking? But Jesus had spoken plainly and clearly about what would happen to Him. How do you suppose Peter could so easily take Him aside to 'correct' Him?

3. How can each of the following become a source of spiritual pride:

    our daily devotional practices;
    relationships with other Christians;
    leadership roles in the Church;
    our witness for Christ;
    knowledge of Biblical doctrine;
    the denomination or church to which we belong?

4. How would you be able to tell when spiritual pride was beginning to creep into your life? Think of the examples of Edwards and Peter. What would tip you off that an enemy agent had begun to make his way into the fortress of your faith?

5. How should you deal with spiritual pride in yourself? In someone else? What advice can you gain from each of the following passages?

Romans 12:1-3; Ephesians 4:17-24; Psalm 139:23f., 24; 1 John 5:1-3; Colossians 3:16f.

3.

The Right Man By Our Side

Did we in our own strength confide,
our striving would be losing;
were not the right man on our side,
the man of God's own choosing.

*At my first answer no man stood with me, but all men
forsook me.... Notwithstanding the Lord stood with
me ... (2 Tim. 4:16, 17).*

When Aleksandr Solzhenitsyn was expelled from the
Soviet Union in 1974, he was the darling of the Western
liberal press. In his novels of life in the Soviet labor
camps, in particular, *One Day in the Life of Ivan
Denisovich*, *Cancer Ward*, and *The Gulag Archipelago*,
the Russian writer had exposed the abuses of socialism

which Stalin had foisted on a helpless nation. Solzhenitsyn's work allowed the Western liberal press to denounce Soviet Marxism as a social and historical aberration, while continuing to hold out the ideal of socialism as a goal worth striving for. Solzhenitsyn was a man of letters, as they fancied themselves to be. He did not suffer fools lightly and had stood up against the political powers of his society and demanded an accounting of their conduct, just as the liberal press sought to do with the governments of the West. His convictions had brought him harassment, condemnation, and ultimately deportation from his native land. He was for many liberal journalists both a living martyr and the vindication of their own callings. He was a hero.

But that was before he spoke at Harvard University's commencement in 1978.

In this, his first major public address in the West, Solzhenitsyn revealed his heart convictions about the state of the West in the closing decades of the twentieth century, what was wrong, where it had gone wrong, and where the West must turn for deliverance. His address was shocking, to put it mildly, and led the Western liberal press to change its view of him, abandoning him completely.

Solzhenitsyn argued, contrary to good socialist policy, that the locus of evil in the West lay not in social and cultural systems, but in the heart of man. He pointed out that, 'though the best social conditions have been achieved in the West, there still remains a great deal of crime'.[1] Western societies had bet on sophisticated social systems, technology, and the human sciences to find happiness and prosperity for all. Their gamble had proven disastrous. Those in the West who still believed that a better world could be achieved through bringing greater government control over the institutions of society were wrong. They had been duped by the press, the greatest power in the West.

Having exposed the lie of socialist utopia and its media cheerleaders, Solzhenitsyn proceeded to comment on what the Russian people had learned from their harsh experience of totalitarian government and a complicit press. Through the suffering foisted on them in the name of socialism, the Russian people had come to achieve 'a spiritual development of such intensity that the Western system in its present state of spiritual exhaustion does not look attractive'.[2] Solzhenitsyn himself, through his struggle with cancer and his many years in the *gulag*, had returned to the Christian faith of his youth, of which he testified most plainly in *Cancer Ward*. His faith helped to fuel a new vision of life and sustained him through the trials and pressures that began to come upon him in the 1960s and '70s. The most tyrannical government in the world might oppose and threaten him, but with Christ by his side, Solzhenitsyn knew he must prevail.

---

1. 'A World Split Apart,' tr. by Irina Ilovayskaya Alberti, in Aleksandr I. Solzhenitsyn, *East and West* (New York: Harper and Row, Publishers, 1980), p. 51.
2. *Ibid.*, p. 57.

In his Harvard address Solzhenitsyn went on to insist that the West was deeply in need of moral renewal. This, he said, was the only thing that could save them from 'communism's well-planned world strategy'.[3] Yet he observed in the West a loss of will power for such renewal and a preference instead for a perpetual status quo of political power and material prosperity in the world. He said this

Did we in our own strength confide,
our striving would be losing;
were not the right man on our side,
the man of God's own choosing.

was 'the symptom of a society that has ceased to develop'.[4] He asked how this could be possible. How could the West, which had thrived on progressive philosophy for decades, have come to such a condition of stasis? His answer was, in effect, How could it have not? For the present debilitation of Western society – its spiritual exhaustion, lack of a compelling vision, and settling into a status quo of material prosperity and the semblance of peace – was nothing more than the outworking and bankruptcy of the Enlightenment philosophy underlying the thinking of all Western societies. This view, which asserted the autonomy of man from any higher being or absolute principles, was bound to end in the dead-end of exhaustion, because men had cut themselves off from their only source of true freedom and meaningful hope.

The West has finally achieved the rights of man, and

3. *Ibid.*, p. 59.
4. *Ibid.*, p. 63.

even to excess, but man's sense of responsibility to God and society has grown dimmer and dimmer. In the past decades, the legalistic selfishness of the Western approach to the world has reached its peak and the world has found itself in a harsh spiritual crisis and a political impasse.[5]

The commitment to 'an autonomous, irreligious humanistic consciousness' was a course that could only end in disaster: 'We have placed too much hope in politics and social reforms, only to find out that we were being deprived of our most precious possession: our spiritual life.'[6] Men did not need more political freedom or economic prosperity. Their hopes would not be realized through more personal autonomy, moral indulgence, or technological sophistication. What the West needed – what the Russian people and Solzhenitsyn had found – was spiritual revival:

> we shall have to rise to a new height of vision, to a new level of life, where our physical nature will not be cursed, as in the Middle Ages, but even more importantly, our spiritual being will not be trampled upon, as in the Modern Era... No one on earth has any other way left but – upward.[7]

The response from the liberal press ranged from condescension to condemnation. Solzhenitsyn's view of

---

5. *Ibid.*, p. 66.
6. *Ibid.*, p. 69.
7. *Ibid.*, p. 71.

life was 'far more dangerous than the easy-going spirit which he finds so exasperating', wrote the *New York Times*. Solzenitsyn had grossly misunderstood Western society, according to the *Washington Post*. His view of life was summed up as 'otherworldly mysticism' by another paper, while others thought him a mere reactionary.[8] Solzhenitsyn had stood alone, with the Right Man by his side, on one of the most public platforms of the nation, and had condemned its most cherished ideals and most popular practices. He had promoted a view of personal and social renewal which ran altogether contrary to the modernist thinking of his Harvard audience and of the liberal press which would report his address. Having denounced all efforts to save ourselves by our own strength, Solzhenitsyn had called the West to return to God, to admit its moral and spiritual bankruptcy and to seek renewal from above, not from within. He had spoken his heart and challenged the Western mind; for his pains he was denounced and forsaken.

The Apostle Paul shared a similar experience in his trial before the Emperor of Rome. The details of his defense ('answer', KJV) are not recorded, but we can reconstruct them based on what we find elsewhere. Paul was taken to Rome to stand trial on charges ranging from heresy to sedition. A preliminary hearing in Jerusalem had come to an abortive conclusion when a

---

8. All references cited in D. M. Thomas, *Alexander Solzhenitsyn: A Century in His Life* (New York: St. Martin's Press, 1998), p. 462.

factional dispute erupted.[9] Subsequent trials before Roman provincial officials had failed to conclude the matter.[10] Fearing a return to Jerusalem and prosecution by an unjust court, Paul exercised his right as a Roman citizen and appealed for a hearing before Caesar. So he was transported to Rome, where, in due course, he appeared to make his defense before the mightiest political authority on earth.

He stood alone, without advocate or friend, before the highest court in the world. His remarks were undoubtedly cordial, pointed, and brief. He paid his respects to the Emperor, summarized the charges against him, and proclaimed them false, especially in view of the fact that not a single one of his accusers had bothered to show up to prosecute their case. He would then have given a brief account of his own experience, how he, a devout and zealous member of the Jewish religious leadership, had persecuted a new 'Way' that had arisen, dragging its adherents off to prison to await prosecution under the charge of heresy. At a critical moment in his life he had been accosted by a revelation from heaven, by which he had come to see the error of his way and the truth of the claims of those he had formerly pursued. His 'crime', as he would have explained it, was that he proclaimed the resurrection of the dead and a new era of the Spirit, in which God had established His King in heaven on high, and was now calling all men to repent of

9. Acts 23:1-10.
10. Acts 24–26.

their rebellion against Him and embrace the One Who had risen from the dead for man's salvation. As foolish as his views might seem to the Emperor, daily embroiled in the duties of governing a disintegrating empire, they were the only hope of men for real meaning, peace, and joy in this life, and everlasting bliss in the age to come.

His testimony finished, Paul would have been dismissed and remanded to house arrest to await the Emperor's verdict. In a subsequent report to one of his ministry colleagues, Paul explained how he had managed to persuade the Emperor of his innocence and to be acquitted of the charges against him:

> At my first answer no man stood with me, but all *men* forsook me: *I pray God* that it may not be laid to their charge. Notwithstanding the Lord stood with me, and strengthened me; that by me the preaching might be fully known, and *that* all the Gentiles might hear: and I was delivered out of the mouth of the lion.[11]

The Lord had stood with him and had secured his acquittal and release. His message was distinctly spiritual, confounding the imperial court and leaving it with no recourse but to dismiss the case. It would be another generation before Roman Emperors would come to understand the full implications of Paul's message and begin to act, often violently, against its proponents. Perhaps the Emperor concluded that Paul's religious

---

11. 2 Timothy 4:16, 17.

message was irrelevant to the concerns of civic justice. Maybe he thought the preacher mad. Clearly, like the Western press responding to Solzhenitsyn, he did not take seriously the proclamation of a new Kingdom and the primacy of spiritual concerns as mankind's only hope in a decaying and dying world.

Yet upon his deliverance 'out of the mouth of the lion' Paul continued to proclaim this 'foolish' ideal in the confident belief that it was the only hope of salvation for mankind. He did not adjust his message or alter his tactics to ensure that Rome would, in the future, give a more favorable hearing to his views. He did not organize a political movement to lobby for legislation favorable to Christians on the part of the Roman Senate. He did not seek to ingratiate himself with leading politicians, nor did he decry the bias of those who had the public's ear in their reporting of the Way for which he stood. He did not turn to any of the contemporary devices of politics or mass persuasion to ensure that his message would receive a more favorable

Did we in our own strength confide,
our striving would be losing;
were not the right man on our side,
the man of God's own choosing.

hearing next time around. Rather, he stood firm in his conviction that the proclamation of the Kingdom was his calling in life, and that the One Who had stood with him before the highest judge in the world would use the foolishness of preaching to accomplish his holy and just purposes among men. As a result, he and the generation which followed his lead turned their world upside-down for Christ.

The same year, 1978, that Solzhenitsyn raised his hands and eyes to heaven and declared that man's hope would only be found there was proclaimed 'The Year of the Evangelical' by the American press. Evangelical leaders had organized for political action. Roundtable discussions, conferences, and seminars across the land considered ways of influencing legislatures and the courts for moral action more in line with evangelical convictions. The evangelical media came to the party, filling the air waves and print with political demands, moral concerns, and strategic advice for the community as a whole. Evangelical pastors and activists met with politicians, lobbied in Washington, raised money for candidates, and sought to influence voters using all the devices of secular political power in what has been thus far an unsuccessful attempt to influence the moral and social agenda in America.

For nearly three decades now the evangelical community has invested enormous amounts of time, energy, and resources into the very strategies and tactics which, as Solzhenitsyn saw it, have brought Western society to a state of exhaustion.

Meanwhile, in evangelical churches, the preaching of the Gospel of the Kingdom languished. New theories of how to reach the lost began to appear, requiring that the worship of God be modified along lines more friendly to the secular mindset, and that the ministry of the Word be changed from proclamation to dramatization and winsome moral exhortation. Within a few years the success of a handful of 'megachurches' seemed to validate this approach to representing the Kingdom of God, and churches of every size and sort began to modify their services of worship and adjust their preaching, hoping to cash in on this latest attempt to make the Church 'relevant'.

With the result that the Church is, indeed, more relevant – to the interests, concerns, and agendas of a postmodern society. At the same time, it has become *less* relevant to the purposes and progress of the Kingdom of God. Confiding in our own strength, evangelicals have sought through marketing, programmed ministries, management techniques, architectural innovation, and secular communications strategies to woo an increasingly indifferent public back to the worship of God. When 'seekers' do find their way to church, what they encounter more often than not is a pale reflection of the world – its music, relationships, and manner of operating – admixed with vague promises of divine acceptance woven throughout a message of spiritual self-improvement focused on the felt needs of a generation desperate for truth. Unwilling to stand on the Word of God alone, the evangelical Church is striving with all its might to win the world on its own terms – striving, but losing, as seems more and more the case.

We in the evangelical community claim to be on the side of Christ, to be serving the interests of His Kingdom and devoted to the cause of His justice, meekness, righteousness, and truth. But by adopting the ways and agendas of the world in our praxis we send a mixed message to our age in flight from God. On the one hand, we affirm its methods and means, its desires and aspirations, thus inviting it to believe that church can be just one more way of achieving their Enlightenment ideal of personal fulfillment, material prosperity, and self-realization. At the same time, we sidestep the issue of sin and point to a myriad of other problems as being the source of our ills – poor self-esteem, want of tactical knowledge ('How to ...'), or maybe just the need of some new friends. With such a message can we possibly expect the Man of God's Own Choosing to stand beside us, as He stood with Paul and Solzhenitsyn? We have forsaken as an offense to our neighbors the message about His blood, His resurrection, His present reign, and His imminent return as the power of God for salvation for all who believe, and we have adopted a message more agreeable to our unsaved contemporaries. Striving desperately not to offend them, we have failed to preach the righteousness of Christ and the requirements of God for holy living. We have called the lost to renewal without repentance, salvation without sacrifice, life without Law. Thus we have offended the Man of God's Own Choosing and are losing any hope we might have had of knowing real revival in our day.

When Martin Luther stood alone before the Imperial Diet of Worms he must surely have thought of the Apostle

Paul before the Emperor. On that long night prior to his final examination, he must have considered tempering his message, lowering his demands, and finding some way of going along with the status quo so as to preserve his position and, indeed, his very life. But, like Paul before him – and Solzhenitsyn and millions of faithful witnesses who would follow – Luther drew on the presence of the Right Man by his side and stood firm with Him. No accommodation, no compromise, no forsaking of his convictions. 'Here I stand,' he declared, the Right Man by his side, through Whom alone we can know true and lasting success.

Think About It

1. When Solzhenitsyn declared his convictions about the need for spiritual renewal in the West, he was denounced and vilified by the American press. Should this surprise us? Why or why not? Have you ever experienced anything like this?

2. Paul wrote, 'For though we walk in the flesh, we do not war after the flesh: for the weapons of our warfare *are* not carnal, but mighty through God to the pulling down of strongholds; casting down imaginations, and every high thing that exalteth itself against the knowledge of God' (2 Cor. 10:3-5). Based on what you know about Paul and his approach to serving Christ, what were those spiritual weapons that he deployed in pursuing the progress of Christ's Kingdom? In what ways are you and your church involved in the use of those weapons?

3. Solzhenitsyn believed – and many others do as well – that the technologies, programs, methods, and agendas of the West have reached a state of exhaustion. Yet the Church continues to rely on these for its mission – ministry programs, approaches to ministry management borrowed from the business world, secular counseling and communication theories, pop music, etc. Is there a danger in this? Why or why not? What Biblical justification can we cite for using such means? What Biblical practices fall by the wayside when we do?

4. Do the Christians you know have a strong sense of having the Right Man by their side throughout the day? Why do you say this? If this sense could be heightened, and if believers could learn to draw more effectively on the Man of God's Own Choosing, how might their lives be different? How might yours be different?

5. What does it look like when Christians are confiding in their own strength in each of the following areas:
- making moral choices.
- daily conversation.
- the way they conduct their relationships.
- their witness for Christ.
- their devotional life.
- participation in worship.

How might each of these be affected by a heightened sense of Christ being at our side at all times?

4.

He Must Win

Dost ask who that may be?
Christ Jesus, it is he,
Lord Sabaoth his name,
from age to age the same,
and he must win the battle.

Of the increase of his government and peace there
shall be no end, upon the throne of David, and upon
his kingdom, to order it, and to establish it with
judgment and with justice from henceforth even for
ever (Isa. 9:7).

We do not remember John Milton chiefly for his theology, which is just as well, given the various doctrinal aberrations that crept into his thinking from time to time. Rather, Milton is revered as the great epic poet of the

Christian tradition, whose majestic blank verse accounts of the redemptive work of God – *Paradise Lost* and *Paradise Regained* – portray the fall of mankind and the saving work of Christ in forever memorable images, characters, and lines.

Yet one of the most powerful of Milton's Christian verses is much less well known among the followers of Christ today. *On the Morning of Christ's Nativity*, first published in 1645, sets forth the meaning of Christ's incarnation in cosmic and eschatological terms, celebrating the Babe in Bethlehem's manger as the Lord of glory Who would vanquish all His foes, 'That he our deadly forfeit should release,/And with his father work us a perpetual peace.'[1] *On the Morning of Christ's Nativity* challenges us to rethink our understanding of Christmas and our approach to celebrating this wonderful season. For, by collapsing the whole of history into an advent narrative, Milton helps us to see the true meaning of this time of year that Christians everywhere hold dear.

The poem is in twenty-seven stanzas of rhymed lines. It begins in rime royal, a strict iambic pentameter rhyming scheme employed by Chaucer and favored by James V I of Scotland, under whose auspices the Authorized Version of the Bible was prepared, and then shifts to an ode, or song, form for the bulk of the poem. In setting his poem this way, Milton tapped into both English literary and

---

1. Lines 5, 6. All citations from *On the Morning of Christ's Nativity* are from John T. Shawcross, ed., *The Complete Poetry of John Milton* (New York: Doubleday, 1971), pp. 63-73.

contemporary Puritan tradition, as well as the popular culture of his day. He clearly intended his work to be read and understood at a popular level.

The *Nativity Ode*, as it is called, begins with a Christmas morning rumination on the events of that Bethlehem stable, in which Milton calls on the Holy Spirit (the 'Heav'nly Muse') to empower him to offer a gift in verse to commemorate the Lord's birth. From this introduction Milton moves on to recount the events of the Incarnation and, more significantly, its meaning and implications.

> But peacefull was the night
> Wherein the Prince of light
> His raign of peace upon the earth began...[2]

Thus from the outset Milton leaves no doubt about the significance of Christmas. Christmas recalls the very day when the Prince of Light came to inaugurate His Kingdom on earth, bringing peace between God and men and vanquishing every spiritual foe. When we consider what Christmas has become for all too many people today, including believers in Christ – the crass materialism and syrupy sentimentalism that dominate the season – we sense that this deeper meaning has been lost on many. As Milton details the appearance of the angels to the shepherds, he can already envision the passing away of sin and hell and the coming of a new day of glory, all as a result of the birth of a Child in Bethlehem.

---

2. Lines 62-64.

However, this will only be accomplished through the suffering and death of the Babe who lies in the manger, and His coming in glorious triumph to judge the world and bring in His Kingdom in its full glory and power. God's Kingdom has surely come to earth in the birth of the Child-King, but only when the last foe has been defeated and Christ is acknowledged as Lord and King of all will His people know the full joy of their salvation:

> And then at last our bliss
> Full and perfect is,
> But now begins...[3]

In anticipation of Christ's ultimate victory the devil is anxious and fearful. We see him nervously pacing the pit of hell, helpless to forestall the heavenly events about to unfold. All the pagan deities and oracles are silent, except to lament their certain fate. It is as though this final Word from God has silenced forever the boasts and claims of false religion and sown

Dost ask who that may be?
Christ Jesus, it is he,
Lord Sabaoth his name,
from age to age the same,
and he must win the battle.

the seeds of its destruction in the coming of His Kingdom. Milton then begins a catalog of the old pagan gods, depicting them as cringing, reeling, fleeing, and ultimately being catapulted into hell along with Satan himself. The coming of the Son of God in Bethlehem thus portends

---

3. Lines 165-167.

the certain destruction of every idol of men, and of the enemy of our souls:

> He feels from *Juda's* Land
> The dredded Infants hand,
> The rayes of *Bethlehem* behind his dusky eyn;
> Nor all the gods beside,
> Longer dare abide,
> Not *Typhon* huge ending in snaky twine:
> Our Babe to show his Godhead true,
> Can in his swaddling bands controul the damned crew.[4]

The foes of Christ 'Troop to th' infernall jail'[5] in utter defeat. The poem ends with a return to the peaceful manger scene, 'the Courtly Stable'[6] where battle-ready cherubim and seraphim – 'Bright-harnest Angels'[7] – sit awaiting their Lord's command. The Lord's ultimate victory and the peace and salvation of His people are complete from the beginning, as the Prince of Light comes to earth in the manger of Bethlehem, routing His every foe and bringing the glory and grace of the Kingdom of God to earth.

The *Nativity Ode* is a truly majestic and cosmic interpretation of the events of Christmas morning, meant to inspire Milton's Christian readers to deeper conviction and greater boldness in their faith.

---

4. Lines 221-228.
5. Line 233.
6. Line 243.
7. Line 244.

This understanding of the nativity of our Lord was not new with Milton and the English Puritans. In the Old Testament the prophet Isaiah was shown a similar vision of a Child Who would come in conquering glory to rule over a Kingdom that would have no end (Isa. 9:6f):

> For unto us a child is born, unto us a son is given: and the government shall be upon his shoulder: and his name shall be called Wonderful Counsellor, The mighty God, The everlasting Father, The Prince of Peace. Of the increase of *his* government and peace *there shall be* no end, upon the throne of David, and upon his kingdom, to order it, and to establish it with judgment and with justice from henceforth even for ever. The zeal of the Lord of hosts will perform this.

Isaiah prophesied during a time of great uncertainty and instability in Judah. The Assyrian threat was never very far away, although God would graciously and miraculously spare His people under Hezekiah's leadership. Just when all seemed lost and Jerusalem appeared ready to succumb to an Assyrian siege, God sent an angel of death among the invaders, causing them to retire in humiliation and defeat.[8] Byron powerfully captured this event in his poem, 'The Destruction of Sennacherib' (1815):

---

8. 2 Kings 18, 19.

He Must Win

The Assyrian came down like the wolf on the fold,
And his cohorts were gleaming in purple and gold,
And the sheen of their spears was like stars on the sea,
When the blue wave rolls nightly on deep Galilee.

Like the leaves of the forest when summer is green,
That host with their banners at sunset were seen:
Like the leaves of the forest when autumn hath blown,
That host on the morrow lay wither'd and strown.

For the Angel of Death spread his wings on the blast,
And breathed in the face of the foe as he pass'd
And the eyes of the sleepers wax'd deadly and chill,
And their hearts but once heaved, and forever grew still!

And there lay the steed with his nostril all wide,
But through it there rolled not the breath of his pride;
And the foam of his gasping lay white on the turf,
And cold as the spray of the rock-beating surf.

And there lay the rider distorted and pale,
With the dew on his brow, and the rust on his mail:
And the tents were all silent, the banners alone,
The lances unlifted, the trumpet unblown.

And the widows of Ashur are loud in their wail,
And the idols are broke in the temple of Baal;
And the might of the Gentile unsmote by the sword,
Hath melted like snow in the glance of the Lord![9]

---

9. George Gordon, Lord Byron, 'The Destruction of Sennacherib,'
in William Harmon, ed., *The Top 500 Poems* (New York: Columbia
University Press, 1992), p. 482.

Against this backdrop of military threat, divine deliverance, and restored peace Isaiah prophesied of a greater season of salvation and rest yet to come.

The images that precede this familiar prophecy in Isaiah 9:1-7 are of a glorious in-breaking of divine revelation and a scarcely imaginable time of peace. The light of God's revelation breaks into the regions around the Sea of Galilee, significantly, that part of Israel occupied by both Jews and Gentiles (Isaiah calls it, 'Galilee of the nations', v. 1). God is bringing the light of truth into the darkness of vexation that settles over the world. That light would come, as Milton noted, in the Prince of Light, Who brings the fullness of God to light among men.[10] This is followed by an image of great celebration, verse 3, as when people realize an especially rich harvest, or when they have spoiled great foes. Next is an image of freedom from oppression – the yokes of

Dost ask who that may be?
Christ Jesus, it is he,
Lord Sabaoth his name,
from age to age the same,
and he must win the battle.

servitude and rods of oppression broken from off the backs of God's people, verse 4. In verse 5 Isaiah envisions a post-battle image, the weapons and garments of warfare are being burned in a great bonfire. So complete has been the victory over the foes of God's people that such equipment will be needed no more. All these images are meant to suggest victory, liberation, and joyous celebration of an unprecedented kind.

---

10. Hebrews 1:1-3; John 1:9.

But they beg the question, How shall this be? Isaiah answers by telling us that a Child will be born, a Wonderful Counselor Who will also be the Mighty God, the Everlasting Father, and the Prince of Peace. The people of Isaiah's day were to understand, as Captain Hook said of Peter Pan, 'This is no ordinary Boy!' The Child to come will be filled with truth from God; He will be God Himself, and will bring a reign of peace to them such as they have never known. He will inherit the throne of David and will establish His Kingdom in justice and judgment, ordering and increasing it without diminution forever. The very power of God itself will ensure the triumph of the Child-King and His Kingdom!

Every year the members Christian churches by the multiplied thousands troop this familiar prophesy out, adorn it with choruses of 'Joy to the World!', decorate their homes and places of assembly, put on their Christmas finery, and go through the familiar motions and protocols of the season.

But Isaiah – and Milton – would have us to see that Christmas, rather than being a season of self-indulgence and sentimentality, is a time for celebrating the ascendancy of God's King to His eternal throne, and of the inauguration of His Kingdom in power, glory, justice, judgment, and everlasting peace. Christmas is the Fourth of July of the Church and should be celebrated with fireworks of heart-felt and glorious praise and thanksgiving, coupled with renewed conviction and greater boldness in service to the King Who still sits on

His glorious thrown to bring His reign of peace and light to all the nations.

But that victory does not come without hard fighting. Christ has captured and put into servitude the demonic leader of the opposing hosts. Now the plundering of his camp may go forward with every expectation of complete victory.[11] But Satan is a stubborn and wily general and has not called his armies to retire from the field. Thus we may expect many skirmishes, attacks, and pitched battles against the enemies of our soul as they endeavor to rob us of our peace and enlist us – wittingly or unwittingly – in their doomed attempt to free their commander and set him on the throne of heaven.[12] Although final victory has been ensured, there is much mopping-up for the saints of God to do as they await the glorious return of their victorious King.

Thus Christmas should be a time of renewing our resolve with respect to the spiritual warfare in which we are continuously engaged. Rather than merely surrounding ourselves with more and more material comforts, observing the rituals and routines that have become all too familiar, and hankering after the good old days of gentle snowfalls on country churches and chestnuts roasting on an open fire, the armies of the Lord should use this glorious season to dedicate themselves to celebrating the victory of their King, arming themselves with the full armamentarium of the Spirit,

---

11. Matthew 12:22-29.
12. Ephesians 6:10ff.

laying plans for the coming year's advance of the Kingdom, seeking out the remaining redoubts of the enemy, and committing themselves to the King and to one another for greater boldness in the battles that yet remain. Christmas should mark the beginning of new initiatives for the Kingdom of God – in our lives as believers and in the communities we serve as the Church of Christ. Christmas should find us realizing a greater fullness of God's Spirit, making more ambitious plans for His glory, and deepening our resolve to know His 'raign of peace' ever more fully. We should come out of the Christmas season not exhausted from its superficial festivities and deeper in debt to the coffers of the world, but renewed in our vision, exultant in our victory, and more resolved and ready than ever to join the battle against the enemies of Christ and His people.

The reign of peace has begun, a glorious Kingdom of light, truth, forgiveness, justice, righteousness, mercy, and grace. That heavenly Kingdom is spreading over all the earth, routing idols and false religions, putting secular and humanistic philosophies to flight, exposing all the lies and half-truths of unbelief, and plundering the possessions of the devil, taking them captive and making them obedient to the cause of Christ. Yet that daily advance does not come without struggle. Christ has won the victory; soon He will win the last battle. For now we, His foot soldiers in the fray, must take up the weapons of our warfare and our individual crosses and follow day by day where He leads, until the last shadow of unbelief and all the remaining redoubts of opposition have been invested, invaded, subdued, occupied, and restored. He must win the battle. This is certain. But we must fight that battle daily in each of our lives, recalling, as Christmas leads us to do, that the Child-King of Bethlehem has become the Almighty Emperor of the worlds Who will never fail us nor forsake us as we go forth in His name.

Think About It

1. What kinds of emotions do you generally associate with Christmas? Are they more retiring or energizing? More placid or stimulating? More nostalgic or more vision-stretching? Why do you think this is so?

2. Milton's view of Christ's victory over idols and false religions has strong Biblical roots. Consider, for example, Psalm 135. How are the enemies of God and their idols depicted in this psalm? Do people still keep idols today? What would be some examples? According to Psalm 135, what can those who keep idols expect of them?

3. Milton and Isaiah challenge us to a different view of Christmas than many Christians seem to hold. It might be said that our current approach to Christmas does more to stimulate idolatry and false religion than the advance of God's Kingdom. How can you see this?

4. For many Christians Christmas is primarily a time of looking back – to the birth of Christ, childhood memories,

and nostalgic sentiments of better days. How does this differ from the vision of Christmas that Milton and Isaiah project? How might you begin to know more of their vision in your own approach to Christmas?

5. Get a hymnal and look at the words to 'Joy to the World!' Do the words of this hymn suggest an approach to Christmas that is more like that of many Christians today or that of Milton and Isaiah? Explain. How might seeing Christmas this way help you to sing this song more like a battle hymn than a nostalgic nostrum? Take a few moments and sing 'Joy to the World!' aloud right now.

5.

We Will Not Fear

And though this world with devils filled
Should threaten to undo us,
We will not fear for God hath willed
His truth to triumph through us!

If it be so, our God whom we serve is able to deliver
us from the burning fiery furnace, and he will deliver
us out of thine hand, O king. But if not, be it known
unto thee, O king, that we will not serve thy gods, nor
worship the golden image which thou hast set up (Dan.
3:17f).

The night was black and quiet, and the sea calm. For
this, Brendan gave thanks to God as he manned the tiller
of the small, leather-covered vessel – called a *curragh* –

that carried him and his companions westward over uncharted seas to preach the Gospel of Christ. In the middle of the sixth century few had dared to venture out on the ocean beyond Ireland's western coast and, of those who had, many never returned.

Brendan had left his comfortable and fruitful ministry in the monastery at Clonfert to follow what he believed was a calling from God to carry the Gospel across the Western Sea to points unknown. It was not an easy decision, but he was determined to go wherever God would send him for the sake of Christ; and if that meant building a leather boat and voyaging westward with a handful of fellow missionary-monks, then that was what he must do.[1]

The voyage thus far had been frightening enough. At a stopping-place where they were generously hosted and re-supplied, a colleague had succumbed to temptation and stolen a precious golden bridle from their host. His death shortly thereafter seemed to Brendan and his men act of divine justice. On another island they had almost been overcome by poisonous waters. Only the grace of God spared and restored them. And just shortly before this dark, portentous night, their vessel had encountered powerful undercurrents that threatened to pull them under the waves. But Brendan appealed to the Lord to

---

1. Complete texts of Brendan's journey, two of over 120 versions of this story to survive from the medieval period, may be found in Charles Plummer, tr. and ed., *Lives of Irish Saints, Vol. II* (Oxford: Oxford University Press, 1922, 1968), pp. 44ff, 93ff.

save them, and the sea 'became calm at once, and the boiling of the whirlpools abated'.

He was exhausted, and, as his companions slept, Brendan let his imagination drift forward to the day ahead. What trials and threats to them and their mission would greet them with the rising of the sun?

Suddenly, just above Brendan's head, a terrifying sound erupted on the mast. Looking up, the Irish missionary saw 'a most horrible, impure, and hellish form'. It was the devil himself, and he was glaring down at Brendan with eager eyes. Startled by his sudden appearance, Brendan gripped the tiller and gathered himself. Was this a vision? A dream? Or was this really happening? 'Why have you come against us?' he asked the fiend. 'To be tortured in the deep prisons of this black dark sea,' came the devil's reply. The blood in Brendan's veins ran cold as he asked, 'What and where is that hellish place?' To which the devil replied that Brendan was sailing right above it at that very moment! Their frail, leather vessel was navigating the very rim of hell! What would keep them from being dragged down, their faith overwhelmed by the terrors of the place of torment? 'None can look upon that place and not die,' the devil cackled with glee at the shaken saint.

The devil had come – whether in a dream or vision, or merely in the saint's imagination – to thwart their mission, to terrify them amid the blackness of night and sea, and to cause them to turn back. He intended that, glimpsing the very pit of hell, their faith should fail and they should either die alone on the ocean or give up their mission. Brendan did not know quite what to do, but he dare not awaken his companions, lest panic and terror break out on board their *curragh*.

All at once the matter was out of Brendan's hands, as the devil drew back the sea and exposed to the missionary's eyes a vision of the torments and horrors that lay just beneath them:

Brendan saw the hard dark prison, full of stench, full of flame, full of filth, full of camps of poisonous devils, full of weeping, and shrieking and woe, of wretched cries and loud lamentations, of mourning and wringing of hands by the sinful people, and the life of grief and sorrow in the heart of pain, in fiery prisons, in currents of ever-blazing streams, in the cup of lasting sorrow and of never-ending unceasing death, in dark sloughs, in seats of fierce flame, in abounding grief and death, and tortures, and chains, and heavy helpless struggles, amid the horrible screams of the poisonous demons, in the night ever dark, ever cold, ever fetid, ever foul, ever melancholy, ever rough, ever long, ever stifling, fatal, destructive, gloomy, bristling with fire, of the lower freezing hideous hell; on slopes of ever-fiery hills, without rest or stay, but hosts of demons haling the sinners into prisons heavy, strong, hot, fiery, dark, deep, lonely, futile, base, black, idle, foul, lengthy, enchanted, ever stinking, ever full of strife, and quarrel and quarrel and weariness, ever dying, ever living.[2]

---

2. Plummer, p.95.

Horror after horror unfolded before him, terrible, fearful sights he had never before contemplated or imagined. Then he heard 'a loud lamentation great, intolerable, unendurable, and a melancholy wretched cry, and a helpless weeping in the depth of the bottom of hell'. Brendan was seized with terror and drew back from the awful sight. Was his mind playing tricks on him? Should they turn back, before all was lost? He shook with fear as he cowered in the stern of the *curragh*, terrified at what might happen next.

'O Christ, will you go with me on the waves?' Suddenly Brendan remembered the prayer of dedication he had offered on a hill overlooking the west coast of Ireland shortly before their departure.[3] Christ, he believed, would be with them at every point of their journey, just as he had promised, and as He had been with the three Hebrew boys in Daniel's prophecy as they stared down into Nebuchadnezzar's fiery furnace.[4] Drawing courage from the presence of Christ, Brendan shook off his fear and ordered the devil to be gone. He had committed himself, his companions, and their mission to the safekeeping of the Lord, and he would not allow some demonic trick to deter or defeat him. The night and sea

And though this world with devils filled
Should threaten to undo us,
We will not fear for God hath willed
His truth to triumph through us!

3. Brendan's prayer is recorded in Robert Van de Meyer, ed., *Celtic Fire* (New York: Doubleday, 1990), pp. 57f.
4. Daniel 3.

became suddenly calm again, like the peace that had come to prevail in Brendan's soul.

The story of Shadrach, Meshach, and Abednego, those three courageous Hebrew boys, loomed large in the minds of Irish missionaries and evangelists during the second great wave of Kingdom expansion that began under the impetus of Patrick and extended for three hundred and fifty years to the end of the eighth century.[5] Their images appear on many of the massive stone crosses in Ireland and elsewhere from the latter years of this period. To the Celtic saints they were a symbol of courage in the face of unthinkable danger and crushing fear.

Their tenure in the service of the great Babylonian king had barely begun when the faith of Shadrach, Meshach, and Abednego was tested in a terrifying and soul-stretching way. To celebrate his greatness and solidify power over his subjects, Nebuchadnezzar had erected a huge idol, commanding that all should bow down to worship it at the call provided by an array of musical instruments. This massive idol was an emblem of an empire filled with devils and demons of all sorts, and Nebuchadnezzar threatened the undoing of any who refused to submit to its demands. At the call to worship, everyone complied. Everyone, that is, except Shadrach, Meshach, and Abednego.

---

5. For an introduction and summary of this period see Thomas Cahill, *How the Irish Saved Civilization* (New York: Doubleday, 1995), and T. M. Moore, 'The Second Wave,' in *Reformation and Revival Journal*, Vol. 8, No. 4, pp. 147ff.

The king had commanded that all who failed to bow down should be cast into a furnace of fire. If they would not obey his royal decrees, their bones would be burnt to ashes, no matter who, no matter their place of service or importance to the empire.

Faithful to their God, the three Hebrew compatriots stood their ground in the face of Nebuchadnezzar's threats, refusing to compromise their beliefs just to save their mortal souls. He could burn them, but Shadrach, Meshach, and Abednego would trust in God to deliver them, whether through the flames or beyond them.

What incredible courage and faith! These were mere boys. They had seen what this tyrant could do. Already he had destroyed Jerusalem and burned the Temple of the living God. He had carried away the cream of Israel's youth to slavery in Babylon, and spread the mantle of tyranny over all of what is today the Middle East and Egypt. Nebuchadnezzar was not a ruler to be trifled with. There would be no persuading or cajoling him. He had threatened to burn them, and burn them he would.

Bound, they were forced up the ladder to the platform just above the open mouth of the man-made hell. From their position they could see the flames and feel the heat. 'One moment,' came the voice of the egomaniacal monarch. 'Heat the furnace to seven times its normal intensity. I want these boys to know the full fury of my wrath.' And it was done. Several of the soldiers who escorted Shadrach, Meshach, and Abednego to the platform became careless, and moved too close to the opening of the furnace. The roaring inferno consumed them utterly, and the three terrified boys could hear the cries of dying men and smell their roasting flesh as the odor of death wafted up and into their nostrils.

'Throw them in!' Suddenly, spears were jabbed at their backs. Strong hands laid hold on them, and they were catapulted off the platform, down toward the gaping inferno below, stumbling and tumbling into the very belly of hell.

But there was no sudden belching of the flames, indicating that they had been consumed. No further odor of burnt flesh came forth from the furnace. No cries of pain and anguish issued from the pit. The king himself mounted the platform to see what had gone wrong. What he saw when he looked into the furnace astonished even him:

> 'Did not we cast three men bound into the midst of the fire?' They answered and said unto the king, 'True, O king.' He answered and said, 'Lo, I see four men loose, walking in the midst of the fire, and they have no hurt; and the form of the fourth is like the Son of God.'[6]

Nebuchadnezzar called into the furnace to Shadrach, Meshach, and Abednego, commanding them to come forth. They obeyed, and stepped out of the flames, to the amazement of the king and everyone present. Not a scorch on their flesh, hair, or clothing. Not even the smell of fire upon them. It was unthinkable. Impossible. Unbelievable!

---

6. Daniel 3:24, 25.

But it was true. And Nebuchadnezzar knew at once what their deliverance meant. Their God had been with them and had rescued them, just as they had declared He would do:

> *Then* Nebuchadnezzar spake, and said, 'Blessed *be* the God of Shadrach, Meshach, and Abednego, who hath sent his angel, and delivered his servants that trusted in him, and have changed the king's word, and yielded their bodies, that they might not serve nor worship any god, except their own God.'[7]

Shadrach, Meshach, and Abednego had, by their trust in God, indeed 'changed the word' of King Nebuchadnezzar. He issued a new decree commanding all people under his rule to worship the God of the Hebrews, Who alone was powerful enough to deliver men from the greatest of earth's kings. It was one more step in Nebuchadnezzar's becoming confirmed as a true follower of the living God,[8] and the end of the brief career of one more foolish idol.

We may not have to face the terrors of hell or a fiery furnace in our daily missions for the Lord. But this world is certainly filled with demons able to strike terror in our hearts and to undo our faith in Jesus Christ. The Word of God calls all those who have come to know the Lord Jesus Christ to join in the mission of proclaiming Him to every creature.[9] The very thought of speaking to a

---

7. Daniel 3:28.
8. See Nebuchadnezzar's testimony in Daniel 4.
9. Matthew 28:18-20; Acts 1:8.

neighbor, colleague, or fellow student about our faith in Christ and the Good News of forgiving grace brings cold chills to the spines of many of us. How can we be witnesses for Him in a day when people are so indifferent, if not outright hostile, to the things of Christ? We'll be laughed at, mocked, talked about behind our backs – or worse. The fear of men prevails over the fear of God in far too many of us, and we prefer to leave the work of evangelism to

And though this world with devils filled
Should threaten to undo us,
We will not fear for God hath willed
His truth to triumph through us!

preachers, missionaries, and those who are otherwise specially gifted or trained. Each time we draw back, hesitate, or refuse to stand boldly for Christ, we are listening to the voice of some first-class demon whispering to our souls, 'You can't do this,' 'This is not the right time,' 'What will they *think* of you?' 'What might happen if you go through with this?' or some other such deception crafted in the furnaces of hell. How much easier it is to avoid the fear of whatever we have decided may lie ahead than to sail on in our mission of making the Gospel known to every creature! But by avoiding the fear – by failing to overcome that fear through trusting in the powerful presence of Christ – we deny our calling, give in to the fear of men, and fall down at the feet of whatever demonic deceiver has persuaded us to compromise our mission for the sake of personal security.

We may praise God for the likes of Brendan, Shadrach, Meshach, and Abednego. They stand as examples of what God can do in the lives of men and women who will not fear the worst that could happen to them as they take their bold stands for Him, but who will continue boldly in faith in their callings as witnesses for Christ. As He was with them, so He will be with all who rely on Him to banish fear, keep their mission in focus, and go with them into danger and uncertainty, confident in His delivering grace. God has willed His truth to triumph over all the schemes and wiles of the devil, and He has willed it to triumph through our witness.

On many of the islands that dot the westward course from Ireland to Iceland, Greenland, and Newfoundland are place-names and artifacts commemorating the mission of Brendan and his faithful troop of missionary-monks. The names of creeks, hills, and points of land, together with the remains of ancient dwellings, remind the locals of the courage and commitment of that dedicated band of evangelists who braved a powerful and unknown ocean, and dangers and uncertainties at every point in their journey, in order to proclaim the message of Jesus. These are our forbears in the faith, who, like those Hebrew boys in Babylon, realized that God has willed His truth to triumph through them – and us – to the praise of the glory of His grace. The heritage of their mission has come down to the followers of Christ today. Like them we are called to face the dangers and uncertainties of our own world, fearless in the face of every threat and foe, and to declare the Good News that Jesus Christ saves sinners. They knew that Christ would be with them on the waves and in every fiery furnace. They did not fear to obey Him. Nor should we.

Think About It

1. Many believers experience fear in connection with their faith. Whether that fear comes when they think about bearing witness for Christ, taking on some new ministry in their church, or yielding themselves without reservation for whatever God wants to do with them, it is real fear, and, left unchecked, can throttle the hopes and callings of many a saint, robbing him or her of full and abundant life in Christ. Have you ever experienced any fear like this in connection with your faith in Christ? Explain.

2. How do we deal with such fear? The starting point is to remember that we live in this world as missionaries for Christ. He has left us here to carry on the work that He began of making His Good News known to others. How can you see that in each of the following passages?
John 20:21; Acts 1:8; 8:1-4; 2 Corinthians 5:20.

3. Every believer is a missionary for Christ. This means that we all have our own 'personal mission fields' to which the Lord has sent us with the message of the Kingdom. Who are some of the people who live in your 'personal mission field'? What evidence do you see that they need to know Jesus Christ?

4. Look again at the message that Shadrach, Meshach, and Abednego declared to Nebuchadnezzar, and his own understanding of what the message meant (Dan. 3:16-18, 28, 29). Taking into account the saving work of Jesus Christ, how would you put that saving message into contemporary terms, so that it would make sense to the people in your 'personal mission field'?

5. As you think about sharing this Good News with the people around you, you can expect to know the same fear that Brendan and the Hebrew boys experienced. The following verses can help you learn to overcome that fear and 'sail on' in your mission for Christ. What do you learn from each of them?

Matthew 28:20; Luke 11:9-13; Luke 12:11f.

6.

One Little Word

---

*The prince of darkness grim,
we tremble not for him!
His rage we can endure,
for, lo!, his doom is sure!
One little word shall fell him!*

*And it was so, when Elijah heard it, that he wrapped
his face in his mantle, and went out, and stood in the
entering in of the cave. And behold, there came a
voice unto him ... (I Kgs. 19:13).*

What a long, lonely, anxious night that must have been.
As Martin Luther bent beneath the low light of a single
candle and began to pore over his books and writings
one more time, all the events of the last four years must
have washed over him like a winter chill.

It was mid-April, 1521, and the signs of spring were just beginning to appear across the German countryside. Everywhere the emblems of revived beauty, new life, and reborn hope were sprouting from the ground, on the trees, and in shrubs and bushes. But it must have all seemed inconsequential to Luther, perhaps even a mockery of his present anguish and all-too-certain plight.

A little less than four years earlier Luther had ignited a storm in Germany by openly and aggressively challenging the practice of selling indulgences for the support of papal building projects in Rome.[1] Good, decent German people were being bilked of their precious resources by ecclesiastical hucksters, who promised remission of sins for their departed loved ones in exchange for contributions to the papal treasury. In hopes of bringing about some public debate over this spurious practice, Luther nailed a document on the door of the Castle Church in Wittenberg, containing ninety-five statements protesting the sale of indulgences. Instead of a debate, Luther sparked a revolt. His ninety-five theses were taken down by a local publisher, translated into German, and distributed throughout the land. Overnight Luther became a lightning rod for generations of grievances, complaints, and opportunistic gambles on the part of the German people. Compelled to elaborate and justify his views, Luther produced more books and pamphlets in which he

---

1. Details of the events leading up to and including the meeting of April, 1521, may be found in Hans J. Hillerbrand, ed., *The Reformation* (Grand Rapids: Baker Books, 1964), pp. 33ff.

further spelled out his concerns about the corruption of
faith and morals that he observed in the practice of the
contemporary Church. It was not long before he found
himself embroiled in public debates with accomplished
scholars, the effect of
which was to further
clarify and harden his own
views and rally the support
of still more of the Ger-
man nation to his side. In
June of 1520 a papal proclamation banned certain of

The prince of darkness grim,
we tremble not for him!
His rage we can endure,
for, lo!, his doom is sure!
One little word shall fell him!

Luther's written works and threatened him with excommunication if he failed to recant. In December of that
year Luther and others burned a copy of the proclamation
in a public bonfire in Wittenberg, along with other books
which they considered full of error. The following spring
the Emperor Charles V summoned Luther to appear before a hearing of civil and ecclesiastical authorities in
the city of Worms, to give account of his conduct, and to
be offered one more opportunity to recant.

The atmosphere in Worms that week in April was more
like that of a carnival than a formal hearing. Crowds
flooded into the city and pushed and shoved for seats to
watch the proceedings, while every kind of peddler
worked the streets without, trying to make 'an easy mark'.
Inside the great public hall, the hearing was solemn and
deadly serious. Shown his books and asked to confirm
that they were his, Luther did so. He was then asked if he

would recant. He replied, 'Most gracious Emperor and gracious lords and rulers, this matter is important and significant. I cannot give, at this time, an answer concerning the books. I pray to be given time to consider it.'[2] His request was granted – for one more day. Although Luther does not provide any details of his study that night, we can be certain that he was very careful to make sure he had said what he meant and meant what he said, and that, to the best of his ability, his words reflected nothing more or less than the clear teaching of the Word of God. In the semi-darkness of his private room he certainly must have reflected on the implications of what would transpire on the morrow. His writings had already been condemned. He had been threatened with excommunication. If he could not satisfy the Emperor, he would surely be regarded as fair game for any assassins willing to strike him down for the reward which would surely be posted throughout the Empire.

Luther was a dead man, and he knew it. One little word would save him: To the question, 'Do you recant?' he had only to say, 'Yes.'

Yet one Greater Word constrained him otherwise. A local reporter, observing the proceedings, took down these as Martin Luther's final words to the Imperial Court:

> Unless I am convinced by Scripture or by evident reason (for I trust neither in popes nor in councils alone, since it is obvious that they have often erred

2. *Ibid.*, p. 93.

and contradicted themselves) I am convicted by the Scripture which I have mentioned and my conscience is captive to the Word of God. Therefore I cannot and will not recant, since it is difficult, unprofitable and dangerous indeed to do anything against one's conscience. God help me. Amen.[3]

'My conscience is captive to the Word of God.' He would be removed from his teaching post at the University of Wittenberg. The Word of God would supply all his needs. He would be excommunicated from the Church, cut off from friends and colleagues and banished like a common criminal. The Word of God would sustain him. He would be hunted, a man convicted of high crimes, and slaughtered without mercy by soldiers, bounty hunters, or ordinary murderers. Yet God's Word would save and deliver him into an eternal rest. Confidence in the Word of God would give this Augustinian monk the strength to face deposition, dis-fellowship, deprivation, and death. That Word was sufficient for Him.

Elijah faced a similar situation in his own dark cave in I Kings 19. Having embarrassed a powerful queen by humiliating and then presiding over the slaughter of her gruesome, wretched priests, he had incurred her wrath. She threatened to bring all the power of her royal position to bear on the task of destroying the meddlesome prophet. In fear for his life, Elijah fled to the farthest point south in friendly territory, Beersheba in Judah,

---

3. *Ibid.*, p. 91.

where he asked the Lord to take his life before Jezebel could catch up to him.

Exhausted, he lay down beneath a juniper tree to await the Lord's deliverance. Perhaps he hoped to die in his sleep and be carried away to the bosom of Abraham without strife or pain? But in the middle of the night an angel awoke him and instructed him to eat. A fire had been kindled nearby, and a wholesome cake was baking on it. A vessel of water stood beside it. From where had these generous gifts come, out there in the middle of a wilderness? He ate and drank his fill, then lay back down to sleep.

But the angel came a second time and told him to eat more, for he would soon be taking a long journey. So death is not to be? What then?

He ate enough to sustain him for forty days and nights, then, in obedience to God's instructions, set off for Mt. Horeb, much further to the south, in much more desolate territory – the very mountain where God had met with Moses following the deliverance from Egypt. What could God possibly have in mind?

There, in a fit of self-pity, he waited to see what God would do or say. Terrifying manifestations of wind, earthquake, and fire buffeted the mountain outside Elijah's lonely cave. Was this the end? Was God coming to annihilate and carry him off?

Yet these powerful omens were but reminders of the way God had appeared on this same mountain to the people of Israel many generations before.[4] As terrifying

---

4. Exodus 24:15-18.

as they must have been, they were but precursors to a more powerful display yet to come:

> And, behold, the LORD passed by, and a great and strong wind rent the mountains, and brake in pieces the rocks before the LORD; *but* the LORD *was* not in the wind: and after the wind an earthquake; *but* the LORD *was* not in the earthquake: and after the earthquake a fire; *but* the LORD was not in the fire: and after the fire a still small voice (I Kgs. 19:11f).

The Lord was not in the raging power and might of storm, earthquake, and fire; instead, He occupied that little Word to Elijah, telling him what he must do in order to know the blessings of God's protection and to continue the work of His Covenant with the nation Israel. But what a strange, bewildering Word it was! Elijah was to go to Damascus (Damascus? But that's so far away! And I have to go back through Jezebel's land to get there!). There he would anoint a new king over Syria (Syria? What has Syria got to do with me or Your good purposes for Israel?). And he was to anoint a replacement for himself, a man he had never met (A replacement? Does this mean my work – my life – is over?).

One little Word from God and Elijah was more confused and uncertain than ever. How could this mandate make any difference? And how would he find the strength and resolution to carry it out? But because it was God's Word Elijah did not fail to act upon it, with the result that God's plans and purposes continued uninterrupted, and Elijah was carried off in a glorious deliverance to his heavenly home. It didn't matter to Elijah that he could not penetrate to the subtlety and wisdom of the eternal counsel of God. What he had heard, he clearly understood, whether he grasped all the whys and wherefores or not. And since he understood he must obey.

One little Word overcame all the doubt and fear that addled Luther's brain and caused his anxious heart to tremble. One little Word sent a frightened prophet on a mission of renewal and blessing for the generations to follow. One little Word – a Word so powerful that not the armies of kings, queens, and empires, nor the schemes and plots of religious leaders, nor the whole course of history could keep it from accomplishing the purpose for which God had sent it.[5] All the enemies of that Word were felled in a moment, like trees for the harvest, as God's faithful servants took the Word in hand and stood courageously and obediently for what it said.

The prince of darkness grim,
we tremble not for him!
His rage we can endure,
for, lo!, his doom is sure!
One little word shall fell him!

In our relativistic, sensual age, where can we find the courage to stand by our convictions and live consistently for Jesus Christ? How can we know what God wants for us at any moment in our lives? How often we today are faced with situations in which we must choose between

5. Isaiah 55:8-11.

the words of people and the Word of God. People tell us to keep our religion to ourselves; God's Word sends us forth to declare it boldly, joyfully, and at every opportunity.[6] People caution us to relax and have a little fun; don't take your faith so seriously. God's Word calls us to walk in the Light of His truth and to expose wicked deeds of unbelief by our righteous, holy lives.[7] People claim the commandments of God are no longer relevant to our postmodern society; God's Word says not a jot or tittle of His Law will pass away until the fulfillment of everything has been accomplished.[8] People tell us to follow our hearts; God's Word warns us not to trust the deceitful, selfish inclinations of our sinful selves.[9] People say that no one can be certain about ultimate things, that everyone needs to be free to decide for himself what's right and what's wrong. God's Word declares that it alone is holy, just, and good.[10] People advise, even warn, us to deny our faith in Christ, if only for our own good. God's Word says that only those who stand by Him until the end will be saved.[11]

Which will it be, the words of men, or the Word of God? So many times one little word will spare us embarrassment, the ire of friends or family, or some protracted argument we can never win. All we have to

6. Acts 1:8.
7. Ephesians 5:1-13.
8. Matthew 5:17f.
9. Proverbs 3:5, 6.
10. Romans 7:12.
11. Hebrews 3:12-15.

do when told to keep our religion to ourselves is say, 'Okay.' All we have to do when urged to go along with the crowds is answer, 'Yeah.' All we have to do whenever we're called to deny our deepest convictions so that those who are still in their sins can continue in their wicked ways without condemnation or intimidation is say, 'Right.' One little word – will fell us like a rotten tree.

But the Word of God is alive and powerful! Luther knew it, knew it so well that he considered obedience to that Word more precious than his very life. Elijah knew the power of God's Word as well. Even though he might not have been able to make sense out of everything it said, or to understand perfectly its meaning for his life, he obeyed to the letter; for he believed that unquestioning, unhesitating obedience was the way to blessing. One little Word from God and His enemies were hamstrung; His people were delivered; His purposes continued without hindrance; and His blessings reached to countless millions beyond the ones whom He was calling to obey Him.

When faced with a choice between the words of people and the Word of God, one other word is likely to echo in our ears. It will be the voice of the prince of darkness, counseling us to use a little common sense, to ease up, back off, cool it, or otherwise deny the living and powerful Word of God which has been entrusted to us. Tremble not for him. Hold fast the Word of God. Set your heart for obedience. Believe that God's Word will prevail against any and every adversity, and walk in the path that Word illumines for you. God's Word is sufficient for all our needs. One little Word from Him will cause the tempter to retreat, the adversaries of God to stumble, and the glory of God to shine through the lives of His faithful ones, whether in the small or the great things of life. Take that Word to heart; cling to it in hope; follow where it leads; wield it like the Sword of the Spirit that it is. Do so, and you will find the courage of Luther and the obedience of Elijah welling up in you with new power, new hope, and new joy.

Think About It

1. Do you ever find yourself in situations where, like Martin Luther, you have to make a hard choice between obedience to God and submission to the words of people? Can you give an example? How do you deal with such situations?

2. Elijah must have scratched his head over God's Word to Him. It just didn't seem to make sense, given his present circumstances and needs. Does the Word of God ever strike you like that? It says something very clearly but what it says doesn't seem relevant to your immediate situation or need? How should you respond? Why?

3. Review the Scripture verses listed below. For each one, how would you expect to hear a 'little word' from the devil counseling you to take a different course?
Acts 1:8; Ephesians 5:1-13; Proverbs 3:5f

4. Peter tells us to resist the devil (I Pet. 5:8), and James tells us that, if we do, he will flee from us (Jas 4:7). What do you think would be some important aspects of a plan for submitting to God and resisting the devil? How would you put that plan into practice?

5. Luther's majestic hymn, 'A Mighty Fortress', addresses in many ways the question of whose word will we listen to in the course of our lives – the temptations and threats of the devil and his hosts, or the Word of God, that stands supreme over all? How might learning this hymn and singing it throughout the day help you better to follow the Word of God at those times when you are tempted to do otherwise?

7.

Word Above All Earthly Powers

That Word above all earthly pow'rs,
no thanks to them abideth;
the Spirit and the gifts are ours
through him who with us sideth.

For though we walk in the flesh, we do not war after the flesh: (For the weapons of our warfare are not carnal, but mighty through God to the pulling down of strong holds;) Casting down imaginations, and every high thing that exalteth itself against the knowledge of God, and bringing into captivity every thought to the obedience of Christ (2 Cor. 10:3-5).

The history of the Christian Church over the past two thousand years has witnessed several seasons of revival, in which the Gospel has brightened and spread in extraordinary ways for extended periods of time. Such a season of revival was the first half of the period referred to as the early Church, the years between the pouring out of the Holy Spirit on the Day of Pentecost following the ascension of our Lord up to the time of Constantine in the early fourth century. During these 250 years or so the Gospel spread throughout the civilized world, crossing barriers of culture and class, sweeping up in its power men and women from every walk of life, and seeing churches established and beginning to thrive, even against the most impossible of odds.

Similarly, the period of the Irish Revival, 430–790 AD, saw a sudden welling-up of God's Spirit in revival, evangelization, and social and cultural renewal that caught up the tribes and cities of Ireland, Scotland, Wales, and the greater part of mainland Europe. The Reformation (1517–1648) effected similar results, even to the point of stimulating much-needed reform within the Catholic Church itself. The Great Awakening of the 1740's in the American colonies also brought about a great ingathering of new believers, as well as a revived interest in the things of the Lord among those already committed to Him.

Periods of revival – sometimes far-flung, sometimes more local – dot the landscape of Church history, reminding us that God is ever ready to renew His people in their walk with Him and their mission in the world. True revivals typically begin in and are sustained by extraordinary seasons of prayer and fasting for repentance and the renewing grace of God. They are fueled by the uncompromising proclamation of the whole counsel of

God and find expression through remarkable and prolonged manifestations of the fruit and gifts of God's Spirit in the lives of His people. They result in renewed and growing churches, and the influx of new members into congregations of every size and stripe. And they leave their impress on society and culture with such transforming power as to recast values, redirect priorities, and renew whole cities and nations.

Yet even in such periods of true revival our ancient foe can manage to sow seeds of corruption into the Church, tossing sand into the machinery of the Spirit that grinds and wears at the workings of the Body of Christ until it becomes ineffectual at its task, in spite of great exertions. Such may well have been the case of the 'new methods' introduced in the middle of the Second Great Awakening (1800–1830) to maximize the efforts of evange-

> *That Word above all earthly pow'rs,*
> *no thanks to them abideth;*
> *the Spirit and the gifts are ours*
> *through him who with us sideth.*

lists at gathering new believers into the Church. Under this system, codified by Charles Finney, evangelists seemed to put more confidence in such external matters as staging, use of music, the manner of public appeal, emphasis on numbers, and the manipulation of emotions than in the work of prayer, preaching, and the Spirit of God.[1] While the Second Great Awakening gave rise to

---

1. For more details on this observation see Iain Murray, *Revival and Revivalism* (Edinburgh: Banner of Truth, 1994).

many indicators of the reviving work of God's Spirit, it is significant that the evangelical Church's influence in the development of American culture and society had already begun to wane toward the end of this period. The 'new methods' introduced by revivalists began to find their way into normal church operations, consuming, over the next 150 years, a great deal of ecclesiastical energy, but with little in the way of lasting results.

Some have wondered aloud whether the evangelical Church might be experiencing yet another season of true revival today. They point to the ongoing growth of evangelical congregations, while their more liberal and modernist counterparts continue to decline; the appearance of growing numbers of 'megachurches'; a burgeoning Christian culture in the form of schools, media, and popular entertainments; and polls that show a tenacious percentage of Americans who describe themselves as 'born again'.

Such data do, indeed, cause us to wonder. However, we might question whether such phenomena are truly the marks of the Spirit of God as He moves in reviving winds across the Church. Might they not as well be only the grating and grinding exertions of a sand-filled ecclesiastical engine, generating much heat and noise, but ineffectual in accomplishing the work for which it has been built? After all, the evidence in the larger society around us – its culture, values, and way of life – suggests that the voice and presence of the Church are not having the leavening effect in our society that we might expect where grace and truth are prevailing. Grace and truth, it seems, have been cast out and are being trampled under foot in America today in the interest of self-seeking, self-gratifying, self-willed people bent on total self-indulgence at whatever the cost.

In his book, *True Revival*, John Armstrong writes, 'The essence of true revival is that the Holy Spirit comes down upon a number of people simultaneously. The recipients might be a church congregation, a number of churches together, scores of churches and people living in a large geographical area, or even a nation.'[2] True revival is a movement and work of God's Spirit, as He wells up with fresh power in an individual, a congregation, or a community of God's people. Because true revival is a work of God's Spirit we should expect to see some indicators of His presence, clear and distinct witnesses to the working of a power from on high as He brings the kind of newness we can never accomplish on our own strength. Dr. Armstrong identifies six such indicators.

The first he calls 'an awareness of God's presence'.[3] In a period of true revival people become profoundly aware of being in the presence of the holy God. They sense His glory in new ways; fall silent in awe of His majesty; and conform their lives to the demands of His holiness, out of both fear of His wrath and love for Him and His mercy. People who are undergoing revival feel

---

2. John H. Armstrong, *True Revival* (Eugene, Oregon: Harvest House Publishers, 2001), p. 51.
3. The following section, *ibid.*, pp. 52-67.

an abiding sense of God's holy presence among them, making all of life sacramental and leading them to praise and thank Him with greater constancy and consistency.

Second, in periods of revival God's people experience what Dr. Armstrong calls 'an uncommon readiness to hear God'. They are hungry for His Word and give more of their time and attention to reading and studying it, as well as to hearing it preached and taught. Nothing satisfies a people in the midst of true revival like the ministry of the Word of God, and they will allow nothing to get in the way of their 'hearing' God in His Word as often as they can.

Third, true revival brings with it 'a deep conviction over one's sin'. Talk of sin is much in the air, and the people of God search their souls to weed out the last root of iniquity. Preachers call their congregations to heart-felt repentance. Lost men and women are confronted with the demands of God's holy Law. Often the sense of conviction will find expression in weeping for sin, crying out to God for forgiveness, and tears of gratitude and joy.

Fourth, true revival is expressed through 'heartfelt repentance': 'Repentance will be genuine, deep, and life-changing. Sorrow and shame for previous backsliding will fill the minds of believers with incredible remorse and result in dramatic changes in their lives.'[4] Not only is there conviction of sin during a period of true revival, but also a turning away from it to follow the path of righteousness more and more.

4. *Ibid.*, p. 62.

Fifth, the moving of God's Spirit in periods of true revival leads to 'an extraordinary concern for others'. God's people are more frequently in prayer for the lost, more generous in their giving to meet the needs of their neighbors, and exert themselves with greater commitment and energy to bring the Good News of God's grace to the people around them. True revival leads to sacrificial giving and sacrificial living, to new ministry undertakings, and to a stronger sense of community among the people of God.

Finally, we may know we are in a period of true revival to the extent that our efforts for Christ and His Kingdom can be seen to be 'bringing about true change'. Individual lives are dramatically and permanently transformed; social ills are redressed; moral ills subside; new cultural endeavors begin; the entire course of a nation's history can be altered, as was the case in Victorian England following the revival under John and Charles Wesley and George Whitefield.

All these are indicators of the moving of God's Spirit in a season of true revival. No amount of earthly power could bring such effects to pass. Only the Spirit and His gifts, at work in new and more powerful ways among the people of God, can accomplish them. When we see such indicators we may know that God has begun to move among His people, and that we are in the midst of a season of true revival once more.

By these criteria our present experience in the evangelical Church hardly seems to qualify. Where is the deep sense of the presence of God? The eagerness to hear His Word? Deep conviction over our sin? Heart-felt repentance? Growing concern for our neighbors? Profound and permanent social and cultural change? The lack of these indicators strongly suggests that what we are seeing today in the vast exertions of evangelical Christianity is not the moving of God's Spirit. Rather, may they not be the tireless but fruitless exertions of well-meaning men and women as they labor to employ the weapons of the world against the spiritual forces of wickedness in high places?

In our efforts to advance the Kingdom of God have we turned to the ways of the world rather than the Person and gifts of the Holy Spirit? We program rather than pray our churches into activity. We manage them with supervisors and committees rather than shepherds. Our worship often smacks more of the presence of the world than the presence of the holy God. The preaching of God's Word lacks conviction – in many cases, even mention – of sin; our devotional lives are scanty, at best. Our efforts at evangelism are contrived and scheduled rather than spontaneous and continuous. Our teaching aims at the head but neglects the heart and the life. Our efforts at social and cultural change are opposed as coercive rather than welcomed as precisely what our society desperately needs. Our pews

> *That Word above all earthly pow'rs,*
> *no thanks to them abideth;*
> *the Spirit and the gifts are ours*
> *through him who with us sideth.*

are filled with people seeking peace and prosperity for themselves more than the Kingdom of God and His righteousness. Our churches are homogeneous congregations of like-minded activists rather than racially and economically mixed communities of servants. Our congregations compete with and condemn one another rather than collaborate and commune together. We are a byword in the mouths of our neighbors rather than a city set on a hill to which they eagerly come for help.

Paul reminds us that our warfare is a spiritual one.[5] In this spiritual warfare we must fight according to the combat manual of the Lord, using weapons of His devising, trusting in His Word as above all earthly powers to accomplish our objectives, and crying out for more of His Spirit and gifts to aid us in our quest. The Lord does not need our programs, organizational charts, fancy titles, detailed schedules, exorbitant budgets, expansive facilities, marketing expertise, and other earthly powers and innovations to accomplish his ends. He and His Church continue, no thanks to these. And we cannot accomplish the ends He has prescribed apart from utter and complete reliance on Him, as He speaks to us in His Word and guides us by His Spirit.

Not there is no place whatsoever for techniques and technologies borrowed from the secular world to advance the cause of Christ. However, when these become the tail wagging the dog, when we depend on such things more and more and rely on God's Word and the methods

---

5. Ephesians 6:10ff.

it prescribes less and less, we cannot expect Him to honor our efforts. We may indeed achieve some semblance of 'success': church 'growth', new programs and facilities, greater personal peace, higher visibility in the community. But this will not be the kind of leavening and lasting success that reaches to every nook and cranny of society, bringing the transforming grace and power of God to bear on lives, values, and institutions for God-honoring change. Only when we turn to the Word of God, placing it above all our earthly powers, and cry out for more of His Spirit and gifts, can we expect true revival to break out in our midst.

We may sing that God is our 'mighty fortress', but when we lean on the ways of the world more than the Word and Spirit of God, our singing has no reality to it, but just a superficial cultural character, lacking real power and resolve – the kind of devotion-less singing that Johann Sebastian Bach described as 'only a devilish bawling and droning'.[6] But as we learn to take our stand on that Word which is above all earthly powers, and to draw on the Spirit and His gifts, we will find that His mighty power to revive and renew will be active among us once again.

Think About It

1. Have you ever experienced a season of personal revival and renewal? How did that come about? To what did it

---

6. Quoted in John Butt, 'Bach's metaphysics of music,' in John Butt, ed., *The Cambridge Companion to Bach* (Cambridge: Cambridge University Press, 1997), p. 53.

lead in your life? If you have not experienced this, do you have any thoughts about what that may be?

2. Look over again the six indicators of true revival. To what extent do you see any of these at work in your own church? Which of them would you especially like to see more of in your church?

3. Even though they work hard and long, churches may not experience revival because they are depending on the wrong things. What is the role of each of the following in your own church?

- boards and committees.
- budgets and programs.
- centrally-based facilities.
- use of statistics.

How can you be sure whether the use of such things is consistent with 'that Word above all earthly powers', or whether they are just earthly powers that are taking the place of something prescribed in the Word?

4. True revival begins in extended, extraordinary periods of prayer and fasting, in which the people of God call upon Him to revive His Church and bring more His saving grace to light in their midst (cf. Ps. 80). Do you sense any need for revival in your church? Why or why not?

5. How might you help your church to begin preparing for God to bring revival? In what ways would you be willing for God to use you to begin preparing for revival in your congregation?

8.

His Kingdom is Forever!

Let goods and kindred go,
this mortal life also;
the body they may kill:
God's truth abideth still;
his kingdom is forever!

Then answered Peter and said unto him, Behold, we have forsaken all, and followed thee; what shall we have therefore? And Jesus said unto them, Verily I say unto you, That ye which have followed me, in the regeneration when the Son of man shall sit in the throne of his glory, ye also shall sit upon twelve thrones, judging the twelve tribes of Israel. And every one that hath forsaken houses, or brethren, or sisters, or father, or mother, or wife, or children, or lands, for my name's sake, shall receive an hundredfold, and shall inherit everlasting life. But many that are first shall be last; and the last shall be first (Matt. 19:27-30).

The turn of the thirteenth century was a good time for ambitious Italian merchants. A careful, clever, cloth-seller, for example, could expect to make a handsome living for himself and his family, and to be regarded as among the more influential members of the community. So it was a good time for Pietro Bernardone, the leading cloth merchant in the Italian village of Assisi, and for his son, Giovanni, a happy, hyperactive, hurried young man who liked to live well and was always ready for an adventure.

When he wasn't off skirmishing with the local militia or pursuing one of his many youthful diversions, Giovanni – his father called him Francis, because the elder Bernardone loved all things French – helped in his father's business, managing the stall where the Bernardones sold their highly-prized cloth. Francis was an unusual young man. He loved the outdoors and the music of French troubadours. He seemed always to have a song on his lips. He was courteous and respectful to all people, whether wealthy buyers or weary beggars. In fact, if Francis had a fault it was that his *joie de vivre* seemed to make him so restless. He flitted from one activity to the next, like the birds and butterflies he admired so much. He enjoyed to the full everything he did, but nothing quite satisfied his ambitious soul. He was always looking for the next thing to do. To some he must have seemed a mere idler, while perhaps most of the townspeople looked upon him as a happy, friendly rich kid who would one day step into his father's shoes, settle down, and become a useful member of the community. For his part, Francis was always on the lookout for something new and more exciting to undertake.

One day, upon returning from a military engagement from which he had to retire due to poor health, Francis wandered the outskirts of town, frustrated and perhaps a little humiliated (had he come back alone because of cowardice?) that his current adventure had been, well, such a bummer. At times like this Francis would retire to the old ruins of the Church of St. Damian to pray and meditate while he waited for whatever his next adventure might be. This time, however, there must have been something more intense, more earnest about his prayers, for in the midst of his meditations he seemed to hear a voice saying to him, 'Francis, do you not see that my house is in ruins? Go and restore it for me.' G. K. Chesterton reports young Francis' response:

> Francis sprang up and went. To go and do something was one of the driving demands of his nature; probably he had gone and done it before he had at all thoroughly thought out what he had done. In any case what he had done was something very decisive and immediately very disastrous for his singular social career.[1]

To Francis this was heavenly mandate, a Kingdom calling, and he could not deny it. He returned to town and sold his horse and several bales of his father's precious

---

1. G. K. Chesterton, *Saint Francis of Assisi* (New York: Doubleday, 1990), p. 54.

cloth. He then made arrangements to use the proceeds of his sale to buy supplies to refurbish the old broken-down church, considering that his father would be delighted to be able to participate in this latest adventure with him.

Well, not so much. When his father learned what Francis had done, he was outraged, and dragged him before the local bishop for judgment and discipline. Money in hand, Francis stood before the bishop, whose authority he was loathe to recognize in this case. In the presence of Francis' father and his ecclesiastical court, the bishop instructed Francis to give the money back to his father, promising that all would be forgiven. But something snapped in Francis – or, rather, seemed to fall into place:

> He stood up before them all and said, 'Up to this time I have called Pietro Bernardone father, but now I am the servant of God. Not only the money but everything that can be called his I will restore to my father, even the very clothes he has given me.' And he rent off all his garments except one; and they saw that that was a hair-shirt.[2]

Francis left the bishop's court and wandered alone in the woods, wearing nothing more than a crude undergarment. The words he had heard in the vision at St. Damian's rang in his ears: 'Go and restore it for me.' Francis knew that this was a divine charge, a Kingdom calling, and that he must fulfill it. So he began going

2. *Ibid.*, p. 56.

about the streets of Assisi begging stones to help in repairing the old church walls. Each day he would drag his offerings out to St. Damian's and take up the task appointed to him. He became something of a local curiosity, as we might imagine. Surely, people thought, this is just a passing phase?

But it was not. Soon Francis was joined by two others who helped him finish his project. Their collaboration led to a mutual commitment to a life of serving others, free of possessions and the concerns of the material world. In time they were joined by nine more devoted adherents, and this was the beginning of the Franciscan Order of the Roman Catholic Church, an order devoted to caring for the poor, the sick, and the downcast. The Franciscans were mendicants; they wandered the streets and lanes of Italian villages looking for opportunities to preach the Gospel and to serve, accepting only the most meager of gifts to sustain them in their daily ministrations. More and more men were attracted to this life of self-denial and self-giving, and the Franciscan movement grew rapidly.

Let goods and kindred go,
this mortal life also;
the body they may kill:
God's truth abideth still;
his kingdom is forever!

Francis referred to himself and his colleagues as 'The Little Brothers' or 'The Fools of God'. The court fool was the one who was willing most to abase himself for the pleasure of the king. This is precisely how Francis saw himself. Francis now began to discover a new joy, not merely in life, but in the God Who stood at the back of all life, and in the Kingdom of God which embraced the whole of creation – from its most humble forest creatures to the most exalted rulers and bishops to 'Brother Sun' and 'Sister Moon'. Utterly impoverished and devoid of any material aspirations, Francis led his band of little brothers in a life of self-sacrifice for the good of others, caring for the poor and indigent, the leprous and dying, and the lost and downcast with all the resources of love and compassion that flowed to them from the throne of God. Through all his ministry he maintained a joy and peace that was the envy of even the wealthiest and most powerful of men. Francis had entered into the joy of the Father and the peace of His eternal Kingdom, and nothing this world had to offer held any allure for him whatsoever.

In time an order for women – the Poor Clares – and one for lay members was started. Today the Franciscans represent a powerful force for social concern and evangelization within the Roman Catholic Church. All because a restless rich kid was willing to give up the things of this world to pursue the Kingdom calling of God.

'You cannot love God and mammon.'[3] Jesus had made it clear that following Him would bring us into conflict with the pressures and temptations of the world. Our parents might disparage our decision to devote our lives to serving Christ. Would we listen to them or stay firm in our love for the Lord?[4] Unsaved friends would constantly be pressuring us to go places and do things that might

3. Matthew 6:24.
4. Matthew 10:35-37.

cause us to compromise our most basic convictions.[5] Family members would think that we had 'gone off the deep end' into religious fanaticism, and they would implore us to return to our senses and get on with life.[6] Our colleagues would think we were crazy.[7] All kinds of frivolous activities would compete for our time, to consume it for worthless ends.[8] And there would be constant pressure from various aspects of the world for us to indulge in its diversions.[9]

But Jesus' words are uncompromising: We cannot have it both ways. Either we will love the world and cling to its diversions, indulgences, associations, and agendas, or we will love the Lord and give ourselves daily as living sacrifices for His Kingdom.[10] We will serve the interests of our flesh or those of the Kingdom of God. We will be loyal to Christ or loyal to the prince of worldliness.

How hard it is to let go the things of the world! How tenaciously we cling to them; how willingly we allow them to drain our energy, gobble up our time, and distract us from our heavenly calling! Weary from too many hours on the job we have little time left for the work of the Church. Distracted and numbed by the diversions of pop culture we are unable or unwilling to take seriously our Kingdom duties. Sunk in debt we have little to invest in

5. I Peter 4:3-5.
6. Matthew 12:46-50.
7. John 10:20.
8. Ephesians 5:15-17.
9. I John 2:15f.
10. Romans 12:1f.

the work of the Gospel. So dependent on our relationships with lost neighbors and friends, we shrink back from speaking to them about the life of faith for fear of offending. Television, sports, investments, possessions, avocations – all take up valuable time, energy, and resources that might otherwise be devoted to the cause of Christ. How many of us, as we sing those words, 'Let goods and kindred go, this mortal life also', really have a sense of what we're saying, and are truly devoted to carrying through with that commitment?

> ❖
> *Let goods and kindred go,*
> *this mortal life also;*
> *the body they may kill:*
> *God's truth abideth still;*
> *his kingdom is forever!*

A glance at such mundane barometers of commitment as our diaries and checkbooks will reveal where our priorities truly lie. How much of our time is given to the active service of the Kingdom of God as opposed to slavish devotion to worldly concerns? What proportion of our money do we spend on ourselves? How does that compare with what we give to the cause of Christ? We cannot not live in the world – its culture, vocations, roles, relationships, and responsibilities – but we can keep from allowing the world's agenda to determine our conduct in each of these areas.[11] We must take care to meet our physical needs and those of our loved ones, but we must not become so enslaved to the things of this world that we cannot readily relinquish them to meet the needs of our

---

11. Mark 16:16; I Corinthians 5:9f.

neighbors.[12] Nor does this mean that as Christians we may not enjoy the good things that God provides for us in this world, even to the realization of great wealth.[13] Yet we must not so cling to riches and possessions that, should our Kingdom calling require, we are unable to sacrifice them to the cause of God's grace and truth.[14]

Life in the Kingdom of God involves a commitment to seeking Him and His righteousness above all else.[15] It means desiring more than anything the will of God for our lives, and committing ourselves heart, soul, mind, and strength to knowing and doing His will as expressions of gratitude and love for Him Who has graciously saved and made us His own. Francis described life in the Kingdom of God this way in his elaboration of the Lord's Prayer:

> Thy will be done on earth as it is in heaven; so that we may love thee with all our heart, thinking ever of thee; with all our soul, ever desiring thee, with all our mind, directing all our intentions to thee; and seeking thy honor in all things; and with all our strength, employing all the power of our spirit and all the senses of our body in the service of thy love, and in naught else: and that we may also love our neighbors as ourselves, drawing all men, as far as it is in our power, toward thy love, rejoicing in the good

---

12. I Timothy 5:8; Acts 4:34f.
13. James 1:17.
14. I Timothy 6:17-19.
15. Matthew 6:33.

things of others and grieving at their ills as at our own, and never giving offense to anyone.[16]

With such a commitment, such an agenda, and such a way of life – a *Kingdom* way of life – we may expect to see God 'face to face, and have perfect love, blessed company, and sempiternal joy'.[17]

The things and relationships of this world come and go. Our bodies wear down, break down, and will one day die. Nothing in this world is permanent; we will carry nothing of it over into the realm of everlasting bliss and unfathomable peace. Why do we clutch so frantically to these things? Why do we allow indulgence in and enjoyment of this world's fare to blind us to the deeper, richer, abiding joys and privileges of our eternal inheritance? Surely we have not allowed the things of this world – possessions, diversions, friendships, work, and all the rest – to become our principle source of security, happiness, and satisfaction? That would be idolatry, and none of us would want to admit that we are guilty of this.

Perhaps all we need is a clearer vision of God's Kingdom, together with the example of faithful servants like Francis who have taken seriously the calling and promises of Kingdom living and have shown that it is possible to find lasting peace and unshakable joy, not

---

16. Francis of Assisi, 'Exposition of the Lord's Prayer,' in Ray C. Petry, ed., *Late Medieval Mysticism* (Philadelphia: The Westminster Press, 1957), p. 121.

17. *Ibid.*, pp. 120, 121.

through worldly things, but through the experience of eternal verities. God's Kingdom is forever, and forever is, as they say, a long, long time. But, as Milton reminded us, it begins now, has begun already, and is within the grasp of all those who take up the calling to follow Christ in every area of their lives, letting goods and kindred go, as well as, if necessary, their mortal lives, for the sake of Christ and His Kingdom.

'A Mighty Fortress', sung with deepening under-standing and true conviction, can help us to attain that clearer vision and to learn to trust in the sufficiency of God, and not the superficiality of the flesh, for all our needs. He will never fail us nor forsake us. He is the Right Man by our side, Whose Word prevails against all the earthly powers and demonic devices that seek to discourage and defeat us. Knox, Edwards, Brendan, Solzhenitsyn, Milton, Francis, and the leaders of the great revivals of Church history knew the sufficiency of God as surely and truly as did Martin Luther. Following their example, and the teaching of Scripture and the example of its great saints, we may know that sufficiency as a truer and more exciting reality in our own lives as well.

Think About It

I. It is undeniable that gaining, experiencing, and enjoying the things of this world takes up a great deal of the time, energy, and resources of those who claim to be Christians. Why do you think this is so?

2. Francis of Assisi, who had always enjoyed life – nice things, happy diversions, exciting adventures, and all the rest – found even greater joy in giving all that up for the sake of Christ and His Kingdom. What do you suppose it is about the Kingdom of God and serving in that Kingdom that could bring greater joy and peace to a worldly young person like Francis?

3. Take a look at the 'mundane barometers' of your own life – your diary (or schedule book or calendar) and checkbook. What do they seem to indicate about where your priorities lie.

4. Read carefully Matthew 6:24-33. According to this passage, about what kinds of things do people tend to worry and become anxious? Why? Jesus seems to suggest that by so worrying they seem to be missing a larger truth. What is that truth?

5. Jesus says that we should 'seek first the Kingdom of God and His righteousness'. Suppose you were talking with a young person who had just come to faith in Jesus and who wanted his life to be really new, wanted to live for Christ and to know the full and abundant life that He promises. How would you counsel such a young person to 'seek first the Kingdom of God and His righteousness'? In what ways might you need to take your own counsel more seriously?

Appendix:
An Enduring Heritage

Martin Luther's 'A Mighty Fortress' has inspired generations of Christians all over the world to a deeper trust in the sufficiency of God. The sheer beauty, majestic power, and glorious truth of this profound hymn have provided strength, hope, and reviving faith wherever believers have sung it for 'the praise of God and the recreation of the soul', as Bach recommended for all music.[1]

Great composers from Church history, enthralled by the music and lyrics of 'A Mighty Fortress', have explored its inherent power in creative settings of Luther's Reformation theme for a variety of occasions and uses. Two among these in particular, Johann Sebastian Bach and Felix Mendelssohn, have given us enduring treatments

---

1. In Butt, *ibid.*

of this great hymn that can further inform and inspire our use of it in personal and corporate worship. Bach, early in the eighteenth century, adapted 'A Mighty Fortress' for a church cantata to make even more emphatic the message and power of Luther's hymn; while Mendelssohn, composing a century later, used it to celebrate the 300th anniversary of the Augsburg Confession, the basic Lutheran confessional doctrine.

Johann Sebastian Bach is perhaps the most creative, prolific, and powerful composer of church music the world has ever known. Particularly in the works he prepared for liturgical purposes – his oratorios, masses, and cantatas – he has left an enduring heritage of glorious music for subsequent generations of believers.

Bach's church cantatas were meant for use in Sunday morning worship. During his tenure as the director of church music in Leipzig, Bach was responsible to write and conduct cantatas on a weekly basis. Of the nearly 200 of these that remain, 'Ein' feste Burg' (BWV 80 in the Bach catalogue) was one of the most frequently performed during Bach's lifetime.[2] Baroque music, the music Bach perfected, combined rigorous order with wide-ranging variation, using prescribed forms in endlessly creative ways to provide a music of energy, vision, and deep emotional content. A typical church cantata consists of eight movements using a combination of forms – chorales, recitatives, and arias – to embellish

---

2. Albert Schweitzer, *J. S. Bach*, Vol. Two (New York: Dover Publications, 1966), p. 459.

a musical theme and a Biblical idea for instructional and liturgical purposes. Bach's cantatas were geared to the sermon text and congregational hymnody and intended to enhance the proclamation of the Word and enrich the worship experience of the people of God. More like mini-operas than choir pieces, Bach's cantatas were truly sermons in song,[3] lasting as long as 20-25 minutes.

'Ein' feste Burg' incorporates the musical themes and lyrics of 'A Mighty Fortress' in four of its eight movements, numbers 1, 2, 5, and 8.[4] Each time one of the themes occurs it is elaborated and embellished in a new and creative way, following the requirements of Baroque cantata genre.

The cantata consists of four voices – soprano, alto, tenor, and bass – accompanied by harpsichord continuo, strings, and oboe. The first movement is a choral fugue, the successive voices entering in with the various 'Mighty Fortress' themes one after the other, layering the words and music in glorious complementarity and exploring the whole range of creative possibilities in a joyous celebration of confident faith. This movement, which sings the first verse of Luther's hymn, is raucous, jubilant, and bold as it declares the principle idea of the cantata,

---

3. Robin A. Leaver, 'The mature vocal works and their theological and liturgical context,' in Butt, *ibid.*, p. 86; Christoph Wolff, *et al*, *The New Grove Bach Family* (New York: W. W. Norton and Company, 1983), p. 124.

4. Movements 2-4, 6 and 7 incorporate another, lost cantata which is more mystical and reflective in character than the boldly proclamatory 'Ein' feste Burg'.

faith in the sufficiency of God our Mighty Fortress. The mood is one of great excitement as the different voices overlap and supplement one another, spurring one another on and strengthening one another as they declare their common faith together, and ending in a harmonius *ritardando* of common conviction which also portends the spiritual conflict to come. This first movement reflects Luther's true desire – to provide a means for the people of God to proclaim together in their own voices and with individual enthusiasm their trust in God as their Savior and King. In this respect it is significant that Luther's hymn is sung in the first person plural – 'we' – unlike many of the praise and worship songs so much in vogue among evangelicals today.

In the second movement Luther's musical themes glide like a mystical spiritual presence in the soprano voice above a bass aria from the cantata, 'Alles was von Gott geboren' ('All things born of God'). While the bass sings,

> All that which of God is fathered
> Is for victory intended.
> Who hath Christ's own bloodstained flag
> In baptism sworn allegiance
> Wins in spirit ever more.
> All that which of God is fathered
> Is for victory intended[5]

---

5. All translations of BWV 80 by Z. Philip Ambrose, Department of Classics, The University of Vermont, 481 Main Street, Burlington, VT 05405 (http://www.uvm.edu/~classics/faculty/bach).

the soprano explains how such a victory shall be achieved:

> With our own might is nothing done,
> We face so soon destruction.
> He strives for us, the righteous man,
> Whom God himself hath chosen.
> Ask thou who he is?
> His name: Jesus Christ,
> The Lord of Sabaoth,
> There is no other god,
> The field is his forever.

Schweitzer observes the use of a 'tumult theme' in Bach's music in this movement: 'Bach employs a particular group among these "stamping" motives wherever he has to represent the tumult of combat, as if he desired to suggest to the hearer the hoof-beats of the horses and the rumbling of marching columns.'[6] The soprano's plaintive voice cries out of its frailty concerning the weakness of our flesh, strongly suggesting, as the lyrics indicate, our inability to succeed in the warfare that confronts us as long as we lean on 'our own might'. The tumult of warfare is real, and we cannot prevail on our own; we need the Right Man to take His place with us on the field of battle if we are going to win.

The fifth movement, which employs the lyrics beginning, 'And were the world with devils filled,' is sung in unison, all the voices blending in one straightforward and powerful declaration against the spiritual forces of

---

6. Schweitzer, *ibid.*, p. 90.

wickedness in high places that assail us – represented in the instrumental accompaniment – and boldly asserting the saints' resolve to stand firm against them. Schweitzer observes, 'Bach launches a whole army of devils against the divine power':

> The [movement] depicts the assault of the devil on the citadel of God. There peals out a signal formed from the opening notes of the melody, whereupon a host of horrid contorted bodies throws itself on the walls ... They mount, sink back again, recover themselves once more, again make the assault, again fall back into the depths – a wildly agitated mass ... From the battlements rings out the exultant song of the faithful ... After a final effort the furious assault falls to pieces.[7]

The instrumental accompaniment of this movement is particularly active and agitated, suggesting the vigor of our spiritual adversaries, while the resolute unison of the chorus depicts the saints' confidence in the sufficiency of God.

In the final movement the chorus joins together in bold, confident homophony to declare its heart-felt faith in God and its resolve to hope in Him and His Kingdom alone. The themes are straightforward and clear, the lyric easy to follow. We can imagine the congregation of St. Thomas' Church singing along to themselves during this

---

7. Schweitzer, *ibid.*, pp. 78, 246.

final, triumphant chorus. Later in the service, when Luther's hymn would have been sung, the congregation's experience of having heard Bach's cantata would reinforce their own singing and strengthen their conviction of the truth they were proclaiming. A careful and repeated listening to Bach's 'Ein' feste Burg' can enrich our experience of singing this great hymn as well.

Felix Mendelssohn took an entirely different approach to adapting 'A Mighty Fortress' to his Symphony #5, 'The Reformation', which he composed in 1830 as a piece for instruments alone. Mendelssohn, Jewish by birth, was a Christian, and seemed eagerly to have anticipated composing this particular work. We find him in London in September, 1829, looking forward to finishing a quartet so that, 'D.V.', as he puts it (*deo volente* – 'God willing'), he can begin work on his Reformation symphony.[8] The finished work is a history painting in music. The first three movements portray the mood of the German people in the days prior to the Protestant Reformation, while the final movement celebrates the power of God in using frail human vessels for His own glorious purposes and incorporates the themes of 'A Mighty Fortress'.

The first movement sets the mood for the work, a mood of dawning anticipation in a time of turbulence, violence, upheaval, and uncertainty. On the eve of the

---

8. Letter of Felix Mendelssohn of September 10, 1829 in Sebastian Hensel, ed., *The Mendelssohn Family (1729–1847): From Letters and Journals* (New York, NY: Haskell House Publishers, Ltd., 1969), p. 225.

Reformation, early in the sixteenth century, Europe was an unhappy, unstable place. Nation states were positioning themselves to gain political advantage over their neighbors. Renaissance humanism was exposing the corruption of the Church and the folly of many ecclesiastical practices and myths. Periodic peasant uprisings were met with violent suppression as rulers fought to keep their places of power and wealth. Plague was a constant threat, as were the Turks. In the first movement, danger and even violence appear to lurk behind every bar of music. At the same time, intermittent flourishes in a major key seem to portend something better, happier, and brighter which is to come. Yet the overall mood of this movement warns of trouble and violence and makes the listener want to seek shelter from the gathering storm. We feel the fear, the uncertainty that people in those times had to live with, and we may praise God that such is not our situation today.

The first movement ends with a stern, grim fanfare designed to illustrate the firm grip of the powers-that-be – civil and ecclesiastical – over the people of Europe. Change seems unlikely; the *status quo* will firmly and resolutely be maintained.

The second movement stands in stark contrast to the first. It is a brisk, lively, exuberant German dance. Mendelssohn takes us 'to the streets', as it were, setting us down amid ordinary folk who, in spite of the difficulty of their lives, will find their outlets for joy and happiness. Even in the midst of oppression and uncertainty people seek joy, and they will find it where they will. Mendelssohn seems to be celebrating the spirit of the German people, who longed for more than what they were experiencing and held out the hope of better things to come.

Yet this joy is short-lived, as are all the joys of our unsaved neighbors today. Following the exuberance of the German dance the music returns to a more somber mood. Languorous and doleful, the third movement falls like a wet blanket on the joy and hope of the second. Dotted notes heighten the sense of anticipation as people seem literally to be tip-toeing through the times. This movement is very brief, and it comes to no definite conclusion. Rather, the final note is sustained, ever so quietly, while the last movement begins sheepishly beneath it.

The final movement begins slowly, then builds in vitality until it culminates in a mighty, majestic paean of praise to God. The 'Mighty Fortress' theme comes in quietly, meekly, in the voice of a single flute, perhaps the frailest instrument in the orchestra. That voice is quickly joined by two others, walking with it in sweet harmony, as still other voices join the growing song until the entire orchestra is engaged. After an initial climax, driving instruments in the lower register introduce a fugue based on the themes of 'A Mighty Fortress'. The music spreads far and wide and high and low, illustrating the spread of the Reformation across Europe and through every social class. The rhythm is fast and energetic, suggesting a mood of advance, hope, and victory over the oppression and darkness that opened the work. The dance theme reemerges, quietly insinuated and developed, then the orchestra returns to the Reformation theme *fortissimo* for the conclusion. Far and wide, among the young and old, the great and small, Mendelssohn seems to be saying, the Reformation has brought renewal, revival, and a return of confidence, faith, and joy to the German people. The final fanfare – a glorious restatement of the opening theme of 'A Mighty Fortress' – celebrates the greatness of God Who alone is to be praised for His wondrous works.

Mendelssohn's symphony can enhance our appreciation of Luther's hymn and our trust in the sufficiency of God in a number of ways. First, it reminds us that He is sovereign over the affairs of men. Times can never be so dark or seemingly hopeless that He cannot break into our experience and do something new and unexpected. In all the situations of life, therefore, He is our hope and our joy, our strength and our reason for keeping on, no matter the trial or difficulty that besets us.

Second, Mendelssohn invites us to nurture a greater sensitivity toward people in our own time whose lives are filled with uncertainty and doubt. God sustains them with good things, and they are enabled to know seasons of happiness and fulfillment. But their lives overall are pervaded by a sense of lostness. They are without God and therefore without hope in the world. Jesus wept for the lost, and so should we. But He also came among them to seek and save them from their sins. His example in this is instructive for us and the very basis for our being in the world as well.

Third, the 'Reformation Symphony' reminds us that the wondrous works of God usually begin small, with one or two faithful people who are willing to take Him at His Word and risk all for His Kingdom. Great works of God do not appear spontaneously, springing full grown from the head of Zeus, as it were. Even the Reformation which began under Luther had its precursors and forebears – Hus, Savonarola, and the Lollards among them. But the great works of God do begin with people, people of great faith, compelling vision, and willing hearts and hands. In His way and time God will use them to spark the flame of renewal in others, and still others, until a mighty movement of God's Spirit sweeps up everyone and everything in His awesome transforming power. Listening to the 'Reformation Symphony' we should pray, like Isaiah, 'Here am I. Send me!'[9]

Finally, the 'Reformation Symphony' with its brilliant restatement of the themes of 'A Mighty Fortress' reminds us of our debt to those who have gone before us in the race of faith. We are but the most recent generation to have received the baton in this ongoing relay of grace. Are we faithful in our day as they were in theirs? Will our generation and the wondrous works of God accomplished in it be celebrated 300 years from now, as Mendelssohn celebrated the generation of Luther and Melanchthon? Are we challenged to learn more about those great saints, so that we might be further inspired by their faith to obedient service in our own generation?

9. Isaiah 6:8.

A Mighty Fortress

Like Bach's 'Ein' feste Burg' the 'Reformation Symphony' of Felix Mendelssohn can help us to appreciate the inherent power of the music and message of 'A Mighty Fortress' so that, as we sing it again and again our own faith may become deepened and our trust in the sufficiency of God stronger and more confident. These are works that bear listening to over and over. They are an enduring heritage of the faith which, when considered thoughtfully and prayerfully, can help us to enter into the majesty and message of Luther's 'A Mighty Fortress' with greater sincerity and conviction.